Head/ Waters

A LEFT BANK BOOK

BLUE HERON PUBLISHING, INC.
HILLSBORO, OREGON

Head/Waters
A Left Bank Book

Copyright © 1994 by Blue Heron Publishing, Inc. Left Bank Books is an imprint of Blue Heron Publishing, Inc., All rights reserved.

ISBN 0-936085-28-2

Editor: Linny Stovall

Associate Editor: Stephen J. Beard

Staff: Meisha Rosenberg, Cairbre Smith

Publisher: Dennis Stovall

Interior Design: Dennis Stovall

Interior Art: Symbols for water adapted from multiple historical sources

Cover Art: George Johanson, Portland, Oregon

Cover Design: Marcia Barrentine

Advisors: Ann Chandonnet, Madeline DeFrees, David James Duncan, Katherine Dunn, Jim Hepworth, Ursula K. Le Guin, Lynda Sexson, J. T. Stewart, Alan Twigg, Lyle Weis, Shawn Wong.

Editorial correspondence: Linny Stovall or Stephen Beard, Left Bank Books, Blue Heron Publishing, Inc., 24450 N.W. Hansen Road, Hillsboro, Oregon 97124. Submissions are welcome. Material is solicited on the particular subjects of forthcoming books and is read only during the period indicated in current guidelines, which are available on request (include SASE).

Left Bank Books is an imprint of Blue Heron Publishing for its topical, thematic collections of literary fiction and nonfiction. New titles under the imprint are published semiannually. Single editions are US $9.95 (plus $2.50 s&h). Subscriptions (two editions) are available for $16, postage paid. All Blue Heron Publishing books are distributed to the book trade and libraries in the United States by Consortium Book Sales and Distribution, 1045 Westgate Drive, Saint Paul, Minnesota 55114-1065; and in Canada by Orca Book Publishers, Ltd., Box 5626, Station B, Victoria, B.C. V8V 3W1.

"Animals as Brothers and Sisters" appeared in *Living by Water* by Brenda Peterson, Fawcett, 1994. "Flora and Fauna in Las Vegas" is from *Raven's Exile* by Ellen Meloy. Copyright © 1994 by Ellen Meloy. Reprinted by permission of Henry Holt and Co., Inc. "The Lesbian Ocean," reprinted with permission from *The Woman Who Loved Airports* by Marusya Bociurkiw (Vancouver, B.C.: Press Gang Publishers, 1994). "Selway" is excerpted from "Selway" by Pam Houston from *Cowboys Are My Weakness*, with the permission of W.W. Norton & Company, Inc. First appeared in *Mademoiselle*, titled "Call of the Wild Man." Copyright © 1992 by Pam Houston.

First edition, December 1994

Printed in the United States of America on pH-balanced paper.

Contents

Foreword 5

Becoming Water 7
    Susan Zwinger

You Can Be in My Dream if I Can Be in Yours 12
    William deBuys

"We Simply Have to Work With Farmers…" An Interview with Marc Reisner 21
    Stephen J. Beard

The Flora and Fauna of Las Vegas 31
    Ellen Meloy

Dancing to the Rocky Mountain Quick Step 45
    Ken Olsen

Photographs 51
    Aaron Johanson

Drop 60
    Nancy Lord

Flowing 65
    Gary Snyder

The Lesbian Ocean 69
    Marusya Bociurkiw

Selway 75
    Pam Houston

Animals as Brothers and Sisters 87
    Brenda Peterson

Waiting For the Parade #3 100
    George Johanson

Northwest Passage 102
    David James Duncan

Holy Water 108
    Jessica Maxwell

Lana Janine Born Again 118
    Joan Skogan

Learning to Love Sea Level 125
    Rick Rubin

Baptism 131
    Lorian Hemingway

Walking on Water 138
    Ed Edmo

Shapeshifting 140
    Jeffery Smith

Signs of Water 154
Bios 156

Foreword

"When the well's dry, we know the worth of water."

Benjamin Franklin's words proved prophetic when I turned the shower faucet one morning and received the quiet hiss of air. The well gave up its last drop on the hottest day of the summer and the day we were to start work on this book.

If all of the water held in the atmosphere fell to Earth, over one inch of water would cover the Earth's surface.

I read that somewhere. The irony of poring over water facts I'd collected for this edition taunted me all day.

"You can drown in a tablespoon of water."

Thomas Farber noted this in his book *On Water*. (Handy for folks in my situation.) He added that it is different to drown in salt water than in fresh water: you suffocate in the former, you die from heart fibrilation in the latter. A question of chemistry.

A flurry of phone calls, jugs of water borrowed from the neighbors, and three thousand dollars cured our water problem. Two days later, with a new pump nestled at the bottom of our 700-foot well, fun and not-so-fun water facts continued to percolate.

Smoke and air pollution above cities cause water vapor to condense into rain droplets. Smoke and air pollution above Mexico City, for example, attracts so much water vapor that the surrounding countryside is becoming a desert.

Solving our problem took little ingenuity or time. A radically different story portends, however, with the alarming statistics on water quality worldwide and the resulting damage to plant and animal life, and the resistance to change from the gross perpetrators — industry, the military, and governments. As the discussion swells, it seems fitting that

Left Bank Books adds its voice to the flow. So this edition speaks of water — celebrating the beauty, adventures, and sustenance that the liquid portion of our planet provides; but beyond that, "head/waters" indicates a wider view, the discovery of sources or headwaters of inspiration that change our ways of thinking about problems and about ourselves.

You're invited to dive into the wide expanse of our theme: from the politics of water with Marc Reisner (*Cadillac Desert*) who veers from his previous attacks on California's rice growers, when a traditional enemy also changes course; to the influence of rivers on personal growth in Jeff Smith's essay on extricating himself from past drownings; to water as the setting for racism depicted in Ed Edmo's painful memoir on swimming pools; to the search for water in the desert in Ellen Meloy's sardonic Las Vegas tale; to water as killer in Pam Houston's (*Cowboys Are My Weakness*) story of a grueling white-water ride. You can swim with dolphins, get baptized, drown, meet the shysters who sold us a dried up water philosophy, cruise the lesbian ocean, become water, flood cities, and fish for the big ones.

Join us in celebrating water, and deep wells.

— Linny Stovall

Becoming Water

Susan Zwinger

The Apprenticeship, Step One:
    Lie on a large log at the high tide line by the ocean an hour before the highest high tide of the month. The waves will boom below human hearing. Take on the power of the incoming ocean in your bones.
    Take notes from the great cacophony of gulls, terns, cormorants, crows, eagles, and ducks as they spiral around thousands of haystacks out from shore. The ferocious pounding that brings you fear, grants them safety, feeds the richest bird rookeries of the globe on islands off the coast of Alaska and British Columbia and Washington and Baja California. The ultimate movable feast pours down the fjords, channels, rivers, to run south along the Kuroshiwo, endless conveyor belts of organic debris.
    The wave energy absorbed through a 5.5 feet diameter Sitka spruce log polished to marble from winters of storm will pulse into your bones. Choose a log too heavy to move, whose shallow root system splays outward 9 feet in all directions, writhing like Medea's head. In the farthest reaches of its snake-roots should hang macabre seaweed, bits of rope, mangled ships, snarled deck chairs, all limp as dead bodies of sailors.
    On top lie with your eyes closed. The impact of that first wave will make the log sigh. The next, shudder. Well past high tide, the water may still rise and rise, punched shoreward by a storm somewhere at sea. Make sure the upper end of the log has been grounded since last winter. But keep some danger.
    Water will churn under your log into pockets and holes beneath; waves will slam dance and gulp unpleasantly. Water may keep rising far-

ther than the high water line. Make sure of escape. Your universe will be made wholly of sensation. Into you will come the rhythms of Earth: of asteroids hitting, of their explosions, of the periodic wipe-outs of life, of the punctuated equilibrium of evolution. Finally, the Big Bang.

A Great Beast Wave will strike. It will shower you with spray. It will condense under your log which will move slightly on its angry back. You will flip on your stomach and grasp two large roots. You will watch the power knit and unfurl.

Prone, you will ride with John Muir on top of his conifer whipping in a Yosemite thunderstorm. You will sail with Joseph Conrad through angry seas. You may drown with Captain Ahab midst the slash of the great white tail. If you are fortunate, you will find yourself about to go down with Amelia...

Step two:

Go to the downtown library; pull huge maps of your bioregion from the drawer. Carefully trace all the edges of water, all the lakes, all the rivers onto large paper. Do not include cities or artificial borders. Move your pencil slowly, sensuously, knowing that each crook and curve is intimately known by someone who loves it.

Step back. View the waterways of the Earth as dendritic veins. Imagine the humps and lumps implied underneath as those of a muscular lover.

Apprenticeship over, work begins.

Become one giant Earth wave, with a wave length of half the planet, pulled by moon and sun, dragged by friction and gravity. Pile up on one side of the globe, then shudder to a pause and change direction. Swell up under fishermen off Viet Nam, caress skin divers in the Caribbean, strand a cruise vessel in Glacier Bay.

Become fascinatingly deadly. Travel farther north toward the poles, go to extremes. In mesotidal Puget Sound, vary only sixteen feet. At Anchorage on Turnagain Arm, gape thirty-three feet. Rush in on the south and out on the north side of the deep glacial channel creating standing waves, bore tides, walls of vertical churning water four feet high. Make tourists screech to a halt in their cars. Remain totally uncanny.

Try this —

Be born of a woman. Try floating around in a liquid for nine months. Or be a woman and surround liquids and cycles of liquids with an intricate nautilus of flesh. This will be hard for some of you.

Drink eight to ten glasses of water a day.

Wear down entire mountain ranges and dump them in layers. Slice whole mountains in half, leaving chains of faceted spurs up U-shaped valleys like pinking shears. Gouge long grooves in stone like horizontal fluted columns, all the way from Alaska to New Mexico. Carve whole mountains into half domes, then fill the valley with concessionaires and tourists, solo free climbers, bumper to bumper traffic, then wipe the whole mess out again.

Or, gently surround Zostra marina sea grass twice a day. Protect and feed hundreds of thousands of salmonoids, Dungeness crabs, ducks, geese, and the myriad of tiny organisms that form the basis of life. Allow yourself to be named by the Coastal Salish, then by the Danish settlers, then by the Orion Company developers, and then as Padilla Bay...but know that none of them count.

Spread over the wings and backs of the great white Trumpeters who, like Lazarus, have returned from the dead, from near extinction (only sixty-nine) in the 1930s to a healthy recovery. Then glint like diamonds as the giant birds toss you off. Or drip off the wings of cormorants stretching in great black crosses against the bright scintillation of wind across your surface. Feed thousands of Brant geese and other waterfowl for whom you are a vital link.

Or, try this —

Pile up in a huge mound 200 feet high and destroy all of Valdez, Alaska, and half of Anchorage. Toss train cars across town in Seward, Alaska. Crush cities in South America and Asia simultaneously.

Or rise gracefully under surfers and kayakers, carry them along, speaking all the time to their muscles, challenge them, let them know a slight shift in weight or twitch of hips changes direction. Make them mad with desire to be out on you.

Fill human eyes with warm salt brine at least once a month. Let them weep for themselves or their dog or a child. Let them weep for all of the losses on this unusual planet.

Make captaining a ship a religion, not a profession.

Flow in and out of a million tidal pools twice a day, gently surrounding the caves and crannies crammed with delicate hydroids and isopods and nudibranchs. The Sistine Chapels of pendulant chartreuse anemones, purple sea stars, and crimson dorises. Create a biological soup as the basis of all marine life. Fill up thousands of sleek fat salmon and follow them hundreds of miles into the interior of continents. Then disgorge your detritus as they litter the land with the nutrients from the sea.

Or try this —

Fill camp cook pots with small trickles of yourself seeping out from the cliffs, slipping through the mudstone and shale, flickering through ferns, coating grass blades like icicles, propelling off rock lips in white tongues of foam. Become miniature waterfalls. End up as rust colored tannin, a forest sampler of detritus: a forest smoothie.

Steep each different part of yourself in a different plant. Make one trickle licorice flavored, sweet, having absorbed in deep leafy woods the Abrus precatorius, Indian licorice.

Sweet and clear, flow out from the subterranean labyrinths of Mount Olympus' glaciers. Melt with rain's hot blade cut down through the ogives and mill holes, siphoning melted glacier into your underground reasoning. Carry within you microscopic blades of sheared rock called "glacier flour," turn yourself opaque turquoise blue. Flow through the rain forest, filtered by Western red cedar and western hemlock seven feet in diameter. Take into you the communion of leaves, insects, lettuce leaf lichens, ground up birds, essence du marmot, and whatever else it offers. With this soupy-brew nourish estuaries, marshes, and bays.

Liquefy ancient forest and send it swirling far out on the Japanese Current curving sharply toward the Far East with the Coriolis effect of Earth turning. Send it out on the Kuroshiwo, translated "Black Tide," toward Asia in a giant flush. Feel two mile drift nets scraping the life from you to feed an exponentially expanding human biomass.

In your crashing waves, snap together organic particles from yourself and nuggets from the ancient forest like Lego Blocks. Scavenge dissolved organic material from the rain forest, glue them into fibrils of

colloidal (gelatinous) proteins. Loop these fibrils into bacterial clumps. Create with this bacteria the very algae which feeds the entire food chain.
    Benthic Metabolism.

Try this —
    Have poets write about you as if you are alive. Scientifically, it is absolutely true, you are alive. You have a pulse, the waves, and a metabolism, your food chain. A personality, a character, a consciousness, and a sense of purpose. Not just poetically speaking, but within the perfection of the trophic food chain spiral, the balances of life forms, and your tremendous drive toward more and more complexity and away from Chaos.
    In that explosion of foam, build the bulk of whales on a molecular level.

Or this —
    Turn into spray, spin rainbows. Mist down granite boulders over mosses, lichen, and a myriad of tiny yellow columbine, foam flowers, and deep pink shooting stars.
    Or swallow the bodies of sailors, drunken yachters, drug smugglers, expatriates, unwatched toddlers, cement-footed mobsters, disowned spouses, humans who no longer wish to live. Dissolve them all into lovely detritus and blend them back into life. Bless them, recycle them.
    Or drill deep into granite and rip it apart with your bare hands.
    And be sure to delight each new child, and each human being. Follow them down stream beds. Patiently receive into you all the rocks and sticks they throw in. Do not swallow every smooth flat stone they throw at you obliquely: let one or two bounce. Humor them. Let them know in their veins that you both are connected everywhere. Enchant them. And through enchanting, change them forever.

You Can Be in My Dream if I Can Be in Yours

William deBuys

We may be the only people on earth who speak of a national dream.

There is no French Rêve Nationale nor Sueño Mexicano, as far as I know, nor a Senegalese or Iranian or Burmese Dream. And there may never be. It took the extraordinary conjunction of a perception of new lands, free for the taking, with crescent economic and political individualism to launch the idea of an American Dream. World events have not seen the like again. One wonders if the planet could bear it if they did.

From the first moment the Europeans waded ashore on Atlantic beaches to the rhinestones, gated communities, and golf clubs of the present, the theme of American experience has never been to lower one's vision of attainable felicity, as Herman Melville once advised, but continually to raise and revise it, year by year and generation by generation. In America the hope is not just to do better but to *be* better — or happier, wittier, sexier, less balding, more busty. In America we expect the options to be profuse, if not prodigal, and from each generation's profusion of possibilities we reinvent ourselves in terms of the desiderata, economic, personal, and at least once-upon-a-time, spiritual of our era. When these sundry elements are joined in a single, amorphous, and ill-packed whole, we call it the American Dream.

At the turn of the last century, American westerners and westerners-to-be stood poised at the edges of a half-continent of dry lands. Almost unanimously, they conceived their dreams in liquid terms: they would turn the dry to wet and make the desert bloom. Tactics for realizing such dreams might vary. Details of ownership, payment, pace, and priority ran the political gamut and not infrequently touched lunacy, but every economically active white man from John Wesley Powell and Theodore Roosevelt to the storekeepers of Provo and Yuma fundamentally agreed that the rivers of the West should be harnessed and that the deserts should be made into farms.

These empire builders were not so crass as to couch their imperative in purely economic terms, for they considered themselves part of a divinely ordained mission. They were hard at work building a nation and a society where none of its like had been before, and from the outset they swathed their new nation in religious ideals. Accordingly, so that they might more persuasively explain their cause to themselves and others — and, not incidentally, so that they might attract subsidies, boost sales, and lift profits — they cast the business of controlling western rivers in moral terms and wove the idea of desert reclamation into the fabric of the American Dream.

Imagine the circumstances: the soot-covered cities of the east teem with unemployed immigrants — what's to be done with them? An oligarchy of capitalists including Morgan, Harriman, Rockefeller, and Carnegie control the railroads and industrial monopolies and, by extension, the nation's fate — how can democracy be rescued from their icy grip? And the nation's farmers, still its backbone, suffer miserably from low prices and rural isolation. Must they live always at the mercy of the railroads and big money, will the life of the nation, together with its dream of progress and self-betterment, now pass them by?

Advocates of reclamation shouted confident answers to those questions, collectively promising nothing less than full salvage of the teetering American Dream, if not of America itself. Was the nation exhausting its supply of free, habitable western lands, the very resource on which Jefferson had premised the survival of an expanding, democratic, agrarian republic? Large-scale irrigation, said the boosters, would open vast new reservoirs of cheap land for settlement. Colonization of the dry West would create homes for hundreds of thousands, relieving pressure on the cities.

As for the future of the republic, they hauled out the nation's most hallowed rhetoric to maintain that soil-tilling desert farm families would embody Jefferson's model of yeomanry better than any of their predecessors. As anyone weaned on American milk knew, such folk would accept nothing less in the life of the body politic than fair-minded, full-bore democracy. Of poverty there would be none, because the endless desert growing season and the fertility of soils that Providence had held in reserve until now would guarantee both productivity and prosperity. Of isolation and backwardness there would be none, for with high production and multiple harvests, farms might be small and neighbors, therefore, close. No family need live so remotely as to miss the benefits of schools and town life, and none need lack opportunity for the cultivation of manners as well as the soil.

Of the many advocates for irrigation, none was more zealous or more captivated by his own rhetoric than William E. Smythe, a Massachusetts Yankee whose uninspired journalistic career in the Midwest began to flourish once he learned to beat the drum for reclamation. As Donald Worster depicts him in *Rivers of Empire*:

> *He was an unprepossessing man with sad, drooping eyes, lank hair parted in the middle, a beard and mustache above a starched collar: the type, one would have thought, to minister to a small brick church in an obscure village, not take on the role of national high priest of irrigation.*

Smythe's *Conquest of Arid America* appeared in 1899, and skimming its florid pages, one senses that the turn of the century must have got to him. He writes with millenarian fervor, as though for the previous thousand years he had lived in cold drizzle and only the desert sun might now bake him back to life. Like other prophets-for-hire, his passionate apprehension of salvation is deeply personal, yet he does not hesitate to prescribe it for all mankind. When Smythe achieves the full stride of his rhetoric, it is as though he breathes not ordinary air but a mixture of helium, nitrous oxide, and other laughing gases. A desert stand of mesquite suggests to him the "good cultivated orchards" of coastal California. The silt-laden waters of the Colorado become "like a stream of golden dollars which spendthrift Nature pours into the sea," and the deltaic soils of the Colorado Desert represent deposits in a bank, "where, when the hour should strike, the children of men might draw their checks against it and never see them dishonored."

In these effusions, Smythe is trumpeting the largest and most audacious private irrigation project ever attempted — the diversion of the Colorado River into the Salton Sink, which the California Development Company, in anticipation of the feat, had renamed the Imperial Valley. The quotations come from an article published in *Sunset Magazine* in 1900 which Smythe titled "An International Wedding: a Tale of a Trip on the Borders of Two Republics." The trip was an exploration of the borderlands of what was then still called the Colorado Desert, the bleak stretch between the Colorado River crossing at Yuma and California's coastal mountains. Fifty years earlier thirst-crazed forty-niners had straggled across those wastes with blackened tongues, achieving depths of misery exceeded only by the Donner Party.

Accompanying Smythe as "chieftain" of the group was "the indomitable man who sees in the transformation of this mighty desert the crowning work of his life." This was George Chaffey, founder of Ontario, California, and the most famous reclamationist of his day. Also on the expedition was "the efficient engineer upon whose surveys and technical studies the physical plan must be built." This was Charles Rockwood, who by 1900 had struggled for eight full years to find capital for the project. Forget for a moment that Smythe's role, notwithstanding his considerable celebrity at the time, was that of public relations flack. Forget also that the Southern Pacific Railroad, soon to be a major investor in Imperial Valley development, had launched *Sunset* as a promotional rag to encourage migration to California and development of its economy. Forget the ingrained conflicts of interests and inherent corruption of Smythe's literary endeavor, and marvel, for a moment, at his perfect orotundity, his unsurpassed facility, not just to dress a business venture in the garments of national dream, but to take that dream and expand and tailor it until it flattered the shape of money-making like a five hundred dollar suit on a twisted old man. Every word he wrote was blarney, and none of his predictions came true, but Smythe's genius was to give people what they wanted to believe, to divert his rhetorical rivers, not into the desert, but into the headwaters of national mythology.

When he announced the pending international wedding of United States and Mexican deserts with Colorado water, Smythe had already replaced, in his usage, the term *Salton Sink* with *Salton Sea*, a far moister and inviting appellation, if under the circumstances, ominous. (Five years later, as a result of the Development Company's ineptness and greed, the main irrigation heading on the Colorado utterly failed so that nearly the whole surging river flowed unchecked into the canal feeding Imperial Valley. For two years the Colorado flowed down this new channel and into the sink, creating a vast inland lake and nearly destroying all the agricultural development that had taken place up to that time.) Smythe, however, found no fault with contemporary canal-building, which "is done quickly and cheaply in these days by machinery," and he waxed ecstatic in his praise of Colorado River silt, which he said would deposit with every three feet of water "the valuable elements of fertilization" valued at over "ten dollars per acre if purchased on the market." (He did not mention that the water would deposit most of its silt in the canals, making them troublesome and ultimately dangerous to maintain.) As for the oven-like climate, it "is one of the best in the world" both for health and agriculture, and it earns this august ranking not least because it is all but immune to rain: "Really, there is no more likeness between agriculture by dependence on the rainfall and agriculture by irrigation, than there is between the tallow dip and the electric light, or between the stage coach and the modern limited train. The one is crude, the other scientific."

And that science, joined with cheap land, Smythe maintained, would set the farmer free: "What are the economic possibilities of the great empire which awaits the fructifying touch of the waters of the Rio Colorado?... It is to be a new civilization, and its cornerstone will be the little farm." This proposition bears special attention. The problem with farming elsewhere was that in order to have enough land to eke out a living, families lived in relative isolation. The Homestead Act, crafted for Ohio and Indiana, contemplated farms of 160 acres. With each farmhouse an average of half a mile from its nearest neighbor, it was a chore to gather enough folks, in horse-drawn days, to have a dance or organize a church or school, let alone a theater that might bring in some aspirant Caruso.

Desert irrigation, in Smythe's telling, fixed that troublesome problem:

> That little farm is another of the precious gifts of irrigation….
> Twenty acres mean eight times as many neighbors as a hundred and sixty acres; ten acres mean sixteen times as many neighbors. Now the truth is that in such a country as the Delta we shall have all the best advantages of town associations combined with the independence of country life….
> Doubtless, settlement will begin here on comparatively large areas, but it must tend inevitably and swiftly to the very smallest farm unit on the American continent. And through those two factors, which men have sought through all the ages, lies the hope of the new civilization and the new race.

And who will be that new race? Will they emulate the Israelites of the Old Testament and labor for Pharaohs controlling land and water? Hardly, says Smythe, who presses forward the example of a more sympathetic, though equally hydraulic society: "No, we shall have another Holland here, full of genius and enterprise, and sufficient within itself. Nature has made it possible. The aspiration of men will demand it. This will be a commonwealth, and it will be true to its best possibilities."

I have it on good authority that, still today, people in Arkansas will warn you about the danger of drinking your own bath water. What they mean is that one should not take one's own grandiloquence too seriously. Such caution, however, would be lost on Smythe, who, in a metaphorical sense, suffered badly from the sudsy bloat:

> Independent by reason of their wonderful agricultural and horticultural opportunities and brought into close and neighborly association by the small farm unit, men should realize here all the best possibilities of country and of town life. The town man should no longer be a tenant and servitor. The farmer should no longer be a drudge, spending his best days in dreary isolation. In the future civilization of the great Southwest, these two prime factors of society will be brought close together, knowing each other and sharing each other's burdens and benefits.

One wonders what level of cynicism, if any, Smythe felt as he wrote such poppycock. Or if he felt none, what cynicism those who used him felt, for if he was naïve enough to believe his own effervescence, he was used.

His vision was utopian, his dream deeply American. Of course, nothing like it ever came to pass. From the outset, the irrigation infrastructure of the Imperial Valley was built largely with the labor of Mexicans and Indians, not a yeoman among them. (Smythe acknowledged that initial construction would require extra help, and he knew just who should provide it: "There are several worthless tribes of Indians in the Southwest, but the Cocopahs are really not in this class…. They will make a useful class of laborers when the country is developed.") The idea of small farms, on which every hopeful promise rested, was also quickly compromised and soon discarded. Although the valley's first farms may have started small, with time they grew to enterprises of enormous size, which depended utterly — and still depend — on the stoop labor of low-paid, brown-skinned workers.

The fathers of the Imperial Valley never let the family-farm rhetoric of the early days interfere with enterprise or with soliciting huge subsidies from Washington. Even after the American taxpayer funded construction of colossal dams to tame the Colorado (and to settle out most of the $10 per acre silt), and even after the federal government built a new canal, the All-American, to deliver water securely to the valley (the old one had flowed on the Mexican side of the line), the farmers of the Imperial Irrigation District steadfastly maintained that they were exempt from a law limiting the size of farms receiving water from federal projects. The limitation, set at 160 acres, was rooted in the very arguments Smythe and his like had spouted for years, but when it became clear that farm size and profitability increased together, valley farmers sang a different song. The Imperial Irrigation District began fighting for exemption from the acreage limitation in 1929 soon after Hoover Dam was authorized, and did not rest until a definitive Supreme Court decision in 1980 gave it what it wanted. Today the valley is home to industrial agriculture on as large a scale as is known anywhere, and most fields, let alone farms, exceed 160 acres. So much for the inevitability of "the smallest farm unit on the American continent."

Smythe and his fellow advocates for irrigation were never shy about dressing up problematic actions with pretty language. One of the least examined and most persistent of their euphemisms is the very concept of reclamation — does any other society use this coinage except as they have adopted it from us? Reclamation, in my dictionary, means "a restoration, as to productivity, usefulness, or morality." What that has to do with putting water on deserts belongs far more to the realm of religion than it does to ideas about restoration. Western American deserts, of course, are not lapsed farms — they are deserts, dry by nature. Causing them to be economically "productive" or "useful" is no more a restoration or reclamation than would be the building of greenhouses in the Arctic.

The idea of reclamation — as opposed to mere colonization and landscape conversion — gets its vigor from an evangelical view of landscape: deserts are lapsed lands, unloved in the eye of the Almighty; they bear the curse God placed on them when He cast Adam and Eve from Eden, and so they require redemption. From a more modern, turn-of-the-century point of view, their potential as part of the Great Engineer's plan might be said to remain unrealized, with only human action lacking to bring the Deity's purpose to fruition. Depending on who's doing the talking, not just any humans were capable of carrying it off. According to Smythe, who spoke for many, "There are some things which the good God intended that we should do for ourselves. With one hand He points to the river, with the other he points to the desert. A man who cannot take such a hint as that is unworthy to live in a country of extraordinary resources."

In the Colorado Desert, there would be no rape of virgin land. God had ordained the uses to which the kiln-dried wastes and their great river would be harnessed. Only consummation was lacking. Consummation, that is, preceded and blessed by sacrament:

> "In no part of the wide world is there a place where Nature has provided so perfectly for a stupendous achievement by means of irrigation as in that place where the Colorado River flows uselessly past the international desert which Nature intended for its bride. Some time the wedding of the waters to the soil will be celebrated, and the child of that union will be a new civilization."

Two months after the publication of "An International Wedding" a two page advertisement, laid out and presented as through it were an engraved wedding invitation, appeared in *Sunset*. Explicitly referring to Smythe's article, it asked,

> *Do you want a ranch in Southern California?*
>
> *A ranch of first-class soil at the Government price of $1.25 per acre?*
>
> *With a right at small cost to all the irrigation water that can be used?*
>
> *Interested parties might contact the Imperial Land Company, Room 224, Stowell Block, Los Angeles, for a map and further details.*

"We Simply Have to Work With Farmers…"

An Interview with Marc Reisner

Stephen J. Beard

Marc Reisner, the author of three books on environmental issues including Cadillac Desert, The American West and its Disappearing Water, his 1986 exposé of the use and abuse of water resources in the American West, has turned his environmental interests into what he now terms "a kind of profit-making cottage industry." The Sausalito, California, resident is one of the leaders in the Rice Lands Habitat Partnership, an effort to demonstrate the potential for farmers, by far the largest group of water-users in the country, to improve wildlife habitat while also producing vast quantities of food for humans.

"I think we suffer nationally from single-issuism and special interest-itis," says Reisner, himself something of an icon to militant, single-issue environmentalists. "We've lost our sense of community. People want something for nothing. They want to blame things [that have gone wrong] on everyone else and not themselves. That's why I've gotten into the business of consensus building. That's what the rice lands project is all about."

Stephen J. Beard: Tell us about the rice lands project.

Marc Reisner: Well, over the years, I've singled out the four largest water users in California for special condemnation. The number one water user in this state is irrigated alfalfa, number two is irrigated pasture, number three is irrigated cotton, number four is irrigated rice. And after that, 15 million people served by the Metropolitan Water District in Los Angeles.

Now the total value of those four crops, statewide, is on the order of a few billion dollars; by comparison, the value of the Los Angeles economy is somewhere on the order of *three or four hundred billion* dollars, the most valuable regional economy on earth.

So here is the most valuable regional economy on earth, increasingly short of water, while one-third of the flow of the Colorado River goes to the Imperial Valley, only 450,000 acres of irrigated land — and about half that land is used to raise alfalfa, mainly for cattle. This is crazy, this is just absurd. If we were to eliminate those crops — and I'm not necessarily suggesting we do that, but if we did — that's 13 million acre feet of water, enough for virtually every home west of the Mississippi River, indoors and outdoors.

Well, I'd been saying things like this for a number of years, and I was not a popular fellow in places like the Imperial Valley and the Sacramento and San Joaquin Valleys. So, to my amazement, a couple of years ago I got a call from the field manager of the California Rice Industry Association, who said, look, we listened to your argument, we know we use quite a bit of water, but we think we raise a good crop and we think we support a tremendous amount of wildlife. He said, if you took the rice crop completely out of business, migratory waterfowl would be devastated. Why don't you come up and see for yourself?

So on the principle that one should always get to know one's enemies so that one can dislike them even more, I decided that I would. It was the first agricultural group that had ever reached out to me, after I had been vilified, condemned, blasted by everyone from Arizona *Cotton Farmer* to the Association of California Water Agencies, which had gotten to be sort of fun and I'd come to expect it. And then, here was this completely unexpected goodwill gesture from the California rice industry — raising a crop for which I may have reserved special scorn.

So I went to meet with them and they had about fifteen leaders in the industry lying in wait for me over lunch. And they had quite a heat on about what I had been saying about their crop and their industry. But they did convince me that the rice lands, after the crop is harvested and the fields are fallow, become in effect a sort of lower grade wildlife refuge.

Now, you have to understand, California has the most productive rice industry, acre for acre, in the world. Their production just beggars that of the Japanese. If you raise rice in a hot, semiarid climate like California's, you can raise a hell of a lot of it, even though it's a monsoon crop. Rice loves the California climate.

Also, the farmers leave about a quarter of a billion pounds of rice grain on the fields after harvest — they harvest with 90 percent or 95 percent efficiency, but they raise so much rice on some 450,000 acres that the 5 percent remaining amounts to a heck of a lot of food. And waterfowl love rice.

SB: Isn't rice a pretty strange crop to grow in what amounts to a desert most of the year?

MR: Well, the reason they grow rice in that part of the Sacramento Valley is because they can't grow anything else. The story of how rice began in California is really kind of amusing. The first rice farmers were Swedes, who'd probably never eaten rice in their lives. Their ancestors had migrated to Nebraska, mostly because they'd looked at a map and saw that Nebraska was 600 or 700 miles south of Sweden. They figured it must have a warmer climate. Well, they got out there just in time for the great blizzard of 1886 and 1887, which just about wiped out the Western cattle industry. Not to mention these Swedes.

Now not long before, the transcontinental railroads had completed their tracks and had received tremendous land grants they needed to sell. So they — I believe it was the Central Pacific Railroad — had track that went south of the Warner Mountains and debouched into the Sacramento Valley. The railroad people — those wonderful connivers — brought some of these poor, shell-shocked survivors of the Nebraska blizzards to California and showed them wonderful land along the Sacramento and Feather Rivers. There were orchards and row crops growing beans, peas, peaches, almonds — a fabulous bounty of fruit and vegetables. And those guys just raced back to Nebraska and said, in effect, man, let's go!

Whole families came out. Then they discovered that what they'd been sold were not the loamy-soil lands right along the river plain, but the hardpan adobe soils further away. So these poor Swedes planted orchards, and they got waterlogged because neither roots nor rainfall could penetrate the several feet of clay, and they died. They tried row crops and failed. For many years, some of them literally lived as subsistence hunters, because there were so many wetlands and waterfowl. Millions of wild ducks were sold into San Francisco.

Then in about 1910 or 1912, somebody got the idea to try rice because it's grown in similar soils in Asia. They didn't know whether the climate would be right, but it turned out to be fantastic and the rice industry boomed overnight.

So, today, after harvest, when it rains a lot, you have shallow standing water in the fields that becomes explosively productive habitat. A different food chain comes up in the winter time, annelid worms and crayfish and midges, things like that — high protein foods waterfowl must eat in order to migrate successfully back to wherever they oversummer, usually in Canada and Alaska.

After the rice growers explained this to me, I began to have a different attitude toward rice. And then one of them made a comment that really shocked me. At the time, there was a great controversy over what was to be the next great dam built in California, Auburn Dam on the American River, which if built to full scale would be close to the size of Hoover Dam. It was a project environmentalists bitterly opposed, partly because of aesthetics and river recreation, partly because of cost — Hoover Dam was built for $49 million; Auburn Dam, they say, could be built for $2 billion, which meant it would really cost $5 billion or $6 billion — but also because it would dam up a river that's already so seriously overallocated that the reservoir would only fill up during a flood. However, because there have been some enormous floods on the American River, a powerful cadre of Sacramento real estate interests wanted it. Well, one of these rice farmers — a big figure in the Republican Party, friends with the governor, friends with water developers — said to me, why don't we just use our rice acres as a flood control catchment basin, the way they do in China? Why build Auburn Dam? We don't need it.

That was an amazing statement, and I thought, boy, you know if this industry has leaders like that, there's some real promise here. Let's try to nudge them in a conservationist direction, and see if we conservationists can learn to make some concessions on our own behalf.

SB: Is that where they got their water anyway?

MR: No. Most get Sacramento River water. They have some of the oldest and best water rights in the state. Growers in the San Joaquin Valley [farther south and largely dependent upon water from state and federal aqueducts] can be cut back 100 percent during severe drought episodes; the rice growers can only be cut back 25 percent.

Anyway, what's happened is we've put together a coalition called the Rice Lands Habitat Partnership, which consists of the rice industry, the Nature Conservancy — for whom I am a principal consultant — Ducks Unlimited, and the California Waterfowl Association. We're working closely with the Pacific Coast federation of fisherman's associations and the Bay Institute, our fisheries consciences. The idea is to flood about 200,000 acres of rice land every winter to create *de facto* wetlands, and at the same time, decompose the rice straw left over after harvest, about two to four tons per acre.

Now, they used to burn the straw, but after resisting bitterly, they were finally forced to sign on to a law which phases out that practice, with some exceptions, by the year 2000. So, they needed another way to get rid of the straw.

There are alternatives. They could harvest it and turn it into a feedstock for biomass power plants. They could sell it for papermaking, it makes excellent paper. They could even build houses out of it.

But rather than remove all that biomass with all those wonderful nutrients from the land every year, why not return it to the soil by flooding it and decomposing it and creating a tremendous amount of food — and habitat — in the process? That's one of the things we're trying to do.

And in fact, this may be a two-way street, with waterfowl as beneficial to rice culture as rice is to waterfowl. The agronomic studies we've done the last three years seem to indicate that the bigger birds like geese and swans trampling the stubble are essential to its decomposition and integration into the soil. And the droppings they leave! If you've got 50,000 snow geese in a field for a week, that's a lot of shit. Some rice growers are convinced they'll need less fertilizer.

Just to give you an idea of what a progressive farmer can create in the way of habitat, there is a guy named Jim Van Tress, one of those farmers who is a natural, visceral conservationist, who was flooding a lot of his acreage even before the rice stubble burning phaseout agreement. At one time in 1992, on a 2,200 acre spread, he had 200,000 waterfowl on his property, something like 8 percent of all the overwintering waterfowl in California at the time. That's according to an estimate by the Department of Fish and Game. Normally, you see numbers like that only on refuges.

But there they were, because there was so much habitat and so much good food, on a farm that in the summertime reverts to rice growing. Jim Van Tress does a lot of things right. He floods his fields. He's left a lot of wild growth for nesting and breeding. He has a magnificent stand of big old oaks, hundreds of years old. His place is a beautiful looking farm, a synthesis of man and nature. So we are trying to nudge a whole agricultural industry in the Van Tress direction.

SB: Are there any problems in doing that?

MR: The major drawback, or I should say the major obstacle, is coming up with the water. In order to do this right, you have to get that water on the fields soon after harvest, which means probably October. The birds are beginning to arrive in great numbers by November, and it takes several weeks or several months for the straw to decompose, so you've got to put water on your fields by October or November at the latest, but California's rainy season hasn't begun by then. The rivers are low, very low, and there are fish migrations underway. Some salmon, virtually an endangered species, are on the move.

So what happens if so much water is being diverted from the rivers that they're almost dry? Well, last fall, we had our first serious fisheries incident. A run of fish was blocked by a temporary diversion dam put into Butte Creek to winter-flood several thousand acres of rice land. Some of the fish were actually sucked out of the river and died on the rice fields.

It was a bit of a public relations disaster. But the upshot of it has been amazing. We've created a special Butte Creek task force, which includes everybody from the commercial fishermen to the Western Canal Water District, where I had my first meeting with the rice industry, to the Bureau of Reclamation. The [state] Department of Water Resources is also sitting in.

We're devising a plan to demolish as many as six of the twelve little diversion dams on this creek. We want to substitute an underground siphon that crosses the flood plain and perhaps puts fresh flows into the river to attract the fish. We want to screen the remaining diversions and rebuild the fish ladders at all the dams that remain. This is probably going to end up costing $30 million or $40 million or $50 million, but it could be the difference between 200 spring-run spawners and 8,000 — what they were still counting in the 1950s.

Virtually everyone is behind it. The water districts along that creek are organized. The Bureau of Reclamation is spending a lot of money on a feasibility study. The Western Canal District, which would build the siphon, has put aside millions of dollars toward its construction.

In the environmental sense, it's a remarkable example of consensus. And it happened not in spite of, but because of this rice lands project. We learned to trust each other. That's when stuff begins to happen.

SB: Farmers can be pretty stubborn people. What do you think made them come around?

MR: Well, they decided that conservationists could be their best friends. The proof was when the Central Valley Project Improvement Act, otherwise known as the Miller-Bradley bill [which among other things, takes water from farmers, gives it to fisheries and waterfowl, and gives fish and wildlife equal stature with irrigation as a project purpose] was passed in 1992. The rice industry refused to oppose the bill — unlike most of California agriculture — and as a result, they were essentially left whole. They even got money, $2 million a year over ten years, to help solve some of the fisheries problems, study winter flooding and its agronomic effects, and so on and so forth. They'd decided not to ally themselves with the San Joaquin Valley and the giant cotton growers down there who are legally or illegally getting taxpayer-subsidized water and think they have a God-given right to it. I think smart farmers in California have taken stock of things and what they see is that 95 percent of Californians live in cities — most of them in the Los Angeles and San Francisco Bay areas, which are hotbeds of environmentalism — and the newspapers they read are constantly espousing and supporting environmental causes and legislation. And whether they agree with environmental ideas or not, they're going to be fighting a rear guard battle if they just resist all demands for reform. They're going to go down in flames.

Now, there are some farmers who have decided to do that. They're theological about their importance to civilization. As one farmer said on a television show about ten years ago: "You know, the passenger pigeon used to be the most abundant bird in the world and it's completely extinct. Do we miss the passenger pigeon? No. When was the last time you even thought about a passenger pigeon? Will we miss the salmon when they're gone? No." He set his cause back about twenty years with that statement.

I was impressed that the rice industry's leadership walked away from that kind of thinking. And I think they've been rewarded for having done so.

SB: Do you see any possibilities with the cotton folks and the alfalfa folks?

MR: Fewer. I don't see another crop in the West as important to wildlife — certainly not migratory waterfowl. I just don't see a parallel situation, but that does not mean we can't work with other kinds of agriculture. What most people don't recognize is that the best wildlife habitat in primordial North America was not Yellowstone National Park or North Cascades National Park or Yosemite National Park — it was places like the Central Valley of California, the Willamette Valley in Oregon, the High Plains, Ohio, Indiana, Kentucky.

SB: Where people wanted to live, too.

MR: Precisely. Where people want to live is usually where you find the best soils, where you can grow the most food. People or wildlife, we're all animals and we all eat that food.

So if we want to arrest the decline of wildlife, and if we're serious about restoring wildlife populations, we simply have to work with farmers because they own most of what used to be the best habitat. And there are some simple things they can do to create better habitat and better conditions. Basically, all they have to do is roll the clock back fifty years and farm the way their forebears farmed.

SB: Not fencerow to fencerow.

MR: Exactly. And if we need to, then we should subsidize them to farm inefficiently. If they take some land out of production, stop trying to drain that little section that turns into a marsh every time it rains, we ought to just pay them to leave it alone. You can support eighty breeding pairs of mallards on those few acres, and if you multiply those few acres by thousands and thousands of farms, that becomes significant habitat.

You know, the farm subsidy system today is designed to encourage maximum production, and then when maximum production is achieved, to *discourage* maximum production by paying farmers not to grow crops. What we ought to be doing instead of that is paying farmers to restore some of their acreage to an approximation of its primordial, natural splendor. If they lose productivity, then compensate them for that loss.

SB: Is this more of a problem in the West than the East?

MR: Yes, it is. What we did in the West, through government intervention on a monumental scale, was develop a third-world economy based on the unsustainable extraction of resources — groundwater, timber, fisheries, and minerals. Now we're mining the soil, as well. In the San Joaquin Valley, what you have is not the great agricultural operation that's so often described, but rather a mining operation on an immense scale.

Everything is being mined. In normal years, 700 billion gallons of groundwater is extracted annually and not replaced. That's about a million and a half acre feet of water, the flow of a good-sized river. It's mined. During the most recent drought, the extraction was four or five times higher.

At the same time, because of intensive use of chemicals in farming the valley, the water is being poisoned. Fresno is seriously concerned about the quality of its water because of agricultural chemicals.

The soil is also being salted out, poisoned with selenium and boron and other toxic minerals that leach out, mostly because of irrigation. That's also poisoning San Francisco Bay, because the stuff eventually drains into the bay. The soil is deflocculating, losing its structural integrity. Salt does that. And the pesticides are killing so many microorganisms that the soil itself is becoming dead, and without its microorganisms, the soil structure then changes and collapses.

Conventional farm practices are ruining things down there. Permanently. There is land that will go out of production, tens of thousands if not hundreds of thousands of acres. It will probably never be farmed again. And mostly because of Federal subsidies of one kind or another — price support programs, subsidized water, subsidized flood control, ag extension programs, you name it.

It was the Democrats, and I am a Democrat, who came along during the Depression and decided to build giant dams and sell water at bargain rates. On the other hand, it was Republicans who decided to treat the national forests as a corn crop, so they're equally guilty, as far as I'm concerned.

SB: Well, in defense of that era, when it began, it seemed to make sense.

MR: It did seem to make sense in its time, but we should have applied the brakes after twenty years. We really got chugging in the 1930s. We were already building dams in the 1950s that just didn't make any sense at all. Today, almost none do. I'm not saying we shouldn't have built Hoover Dam, I'm not saying we shouldn't have built Bonneville and some of the other dams on the Columbia. *Maybe.* You can make a strong argument that Grand Coulee Dam won the Second World War, because its power produced so many ships and planes. Given the choice between a world under Fascism and a world under democracy, sort of, if a dam might make the difference, perhaps you build the dam.

But all that's irrelevant. When Grand Coulee dam was built, the Second World War was not really foreseen. Grand Coulee was built because the government wanted to build a big dam up there. Period. To hell with the salmon. Dams were now to symbolize the Pacific Northwest. Unfortunately, most of the people in the region thought that was fine. They sure don't anymore.

We went overboard — we usually do. It's the pendulum principle of imperfect democratic society. And now it's going to be tricky and expensive, and to some degree socially disruptive, to bring back some, not all, of the primordial splendor that we just threw in the trash can. But we're going to do it. I think we will. Too many of us want to.

The Flora and Fauna of Las Vegas

Ellen Meloy

> Human domination over nature is quite simply an illusion, a passing dream by a naïve species. It is an illusion that has cost us much, ensnared us in our own designs, given us a few boasts to make about our courage and genius, but all the same it is an illusion. Do what we will, the Colorado will one day find an unimpeded way to the sea.
> — Donald Worster, *Under Western Skies*

Ascent. Summit. Descent. The interstate highway, the asphalt river, slips off the Colorado Plateau, rises and falls over the Great Basin's rhythmic contours of basin and range, and flows southwest toward the Mojave Desert. In basin, the highway crosses the Sevier River, which the 1776 Domínguez-Escalante expedition, ever hoping to find a Pacific passage, erroneously linked with the Green River in the Uinta Basin. Through range, the meticulously graveled and graded highway slopes bury Fremont village sites, their remains relocated to museums to make way for the four-lane. A few petroglyph panels are visible from the road. We cannot study them. We cannot get off the highway. No exit. The panels pass in a blur, ancient peeps drowned by billboard shouts: IT'S THE REAL THING.

The flanks of the Tushar and Pavant ranges tip us into the Parowan Valley, where we nose the truck south into the current of traffic through Mormon farm towns, each with identical, master design brick churches surrounded by weekday-empty aprons of tarmac. Only Kmart has more parking lot. Solid and impervious, the churches may be rocket ships in disguise. When the Rapture comes, the Saints will simply hop in and blast off, smothering the apron in the dense vapor of afterburners without singeing a leaf on God's flora. Near Cedar City I glimpse a road kill that may or may not be a poodle flung from a recreational vehicle. At a rest stop a teenager lifts his muscle shirt and stares at his navel. We're closer, I think. We have entered the gravitational field.

Most of the billboards in St. George advertise Nevada casinos, luring Utahans over the nearby state line to Mesquite or Las Vegas, the pull on their retirement dollar stronger than the pull of their faith. Flanked by the Beaver Dam Mountains and Hurricane Cliffs, St. George hemorrhages subdivisions and factory outlet malls and a lunatic compulsion to have the most golf courses in the universe, irrigated by the Virgin River, soon to be dammed, IMAXed, and deflowered of rare desert tortoises. Perhaps St. Georgians deserve all the golf they can muster. Many are Downwinders, human receptacles of nuclear fallout that scars their lives with seemingly endless tragedy.

During the atmospheric nuclear testing in the Nevada desert west of St. George from 1951 to 1962, it was the Atomic Energy Commission's practice to wait until the wind blew toward Utah before detonating its "shots" in order to avoid contaminating populous Las Vegas or Los Angeles. An AEC memo declassified two decades after the test era described the people living in the fallout's path as "a low-use segment of the population." Loyal to a government they believed to be divinely inspired, taught by their church never to challenge authority, assured by that authority that the radiation was harmless, Utah's patriotic Mormons endured the toxic showers with little objection.

When Utahans and Nevadans reported their symptoms and fears, public health officials told them that only their "neurosis" about the bombs would make them ill. When women reported burns, peeling skin, nausea, and diarrhea — all symptoms of radiation sickness — when they said their hair, fingernails, and toenails fell out after a cloud of fallout passed over them, their doctors wrote "change of life" or "housewife's syndrome" or "recent hysterectomy" on their charts. The dangers of radiation were known but suppressed, a "noble lie" deemed a necessary cost of national security and the fight against communism. Bomb after bomb exploded, some of them, like Shot Harry in 1953, extremely "dirty" and lethal, showering fallout throughout the West. Each nuclear test released radiation in amounts comparable to the radiation released at Chernobyl in 1986. In at least two ways the Nevada tests were nothing like Chernobyl: There were 126 detonations. None was an accident.

At the Nevada state line we cast aside Utah's wholesome aura for its nemesis. Behind: Leave it to Beaver. Ahead: Sodom and Gomorrah. In dusk that sizzles at 103 degrees, the land sprawls in bowls of creosote bush cupped by serrated ribs of rock. Over a long rise, past a convoy of trucks afloat in mirages of diesel and heat, we top the crest of the final ridge and behold the valley below, an island of neon capped in sludgy brown smog, ringed by a rabid housing boom. Las Vegas. The meadows.

We grind down the freeway past warehouses and a cinder block wall over which a life-size white plaster elephant, rogue prop from a theme park, curls its trunk, flares its ears, and rests ivory tusks on the barrier that separates its lunging charge from the highway's shoulder. Oleander bushes, carbon monoxide-tolerant but poisonous in their own right — they once offed a few Boy Scouts who peeled their thin branches, impaled hot dogs on their tips, and roasted a lethal meal — line the freeway then surrender to a chute of concrete, where we fly without air-conditioning in the gridlock of an exit bottleneck, surrounded by chilled limousines and Porsches. No one leaps out to save our lives. The ambient light is pale yellow, like the inside of a banana peel.

Why this pilgrimage from Desolation Canyon, our home on Utah's Green River, to Glitter Gulch, from cougar-blessed red-rock wilderness to the apex of engineered fantasy, from mesmerization to masochism? Why have we ventured so far from the river? Because our river is here beneath our smoldering, heat-frayed, about-to-explode radials. Only in Egypt are more people dependent on the flow of one river than the people of Clark County, Nevada. By controlling the Colorado River through the state's southern tip, Nevadans freed themselves from the constraints posed by puny, ill-timed rainfall that otherwise barely sustained darkling beetles, chuckwallas, and creosote bushes. In this century no place has been too remote or too parched to reach with a lifeline, and the Colorado River, by this point carrying water from the

Green, San Juan, Virgin, and other tributaries, is Las Vegas's intravenous feeding, its umbilical to prosperity, the force that pulsates the neon through the tubes. Here the River immolates its wild treasures on the altar of entrepreneurial spirit. We have chosen to devote much of the West's greatest waterway to this city. Las Vegas is the twentieth century's ultimate perversion of the River and the site of a twenty-first-century water war.

For every river rat this visit is mandatory. We cannot know the River until we know this place. Our pilgrimage also carries corollary missions. I hope to learn what Las Vegans know about their water. There is field research to be done. And I want everyone in the Excalibur Hotel and Casino, a massive, pseudomedieval, castellated grotesquerie with jousting matches, banquets, and 4,032 hotel rooms — *4,032 toilets* — to flush their toilets at precisely the same moment.

I wait in the truck while my husband, Mark, registers at the hotel, the only vehicle-enclosed human in Nevada without a veneer of tinted safety glass between her and the rude assault of Real Air. I cannot go into the hotel because Real Air has fused my skin to the Naugahyde panel inside the truck door. My earrings, a Hopi man-in-the-maze design inlaid in silver, conduct so much heat, they sear man-in-the-maze-shaped burns on my neck.

The second thing Mark says to the waitress as we pump freon through our organs inside an air-conditioned restaurant: "Are you real?" She has a practiced tolerance for stupid questions and a tattoo on her left breast. The menu offers an entree called Heavy Trim Beef Primals. "I'd like a cheeseburger, please, hold the onions," Mark says, Green River sand spilling from his cuffs as he passes her the menu. "Are you real?"

The restaurant seethes with slick-baited bloodsuckers in shark-skin suits on cappuccino breaks from their drug harems and sieges of women wearing very short skirts who should not, Vegas being the one place where they can get away with this. The bun-grazing skirt on the cigarette girl remains immobile as she vigorously diversifies her cigarette-shy market by peddling illuminated Yo-Yos. The diners' sunburns, freshly acquired while powerboating on nearby Lake Mead, radiate sufficient heat to melt the ice in our water glasses. While we played Lost Tribe of the Oligocenc on the river, male strippers became passé and musical revues with full-figured dancers became the rage: SENSATIONAL. TALENTED. PUDGY, proclaims one flashing Strip marquee.

"What are you in the mood for?" Mark asks about the evening's casino crawl. "Knights? Rome? The circus? The tropics? Urban South American festivities?" We settle on the Tropicana, an island-theme concoction whose grand entry sprouts the huge plaster heads of tiki gods from tidy plots of stale-smelling hothouse petunias, ferns, fountains, and sprinkler heads pumping liquid no faster than the desert air can evaporate it. The fountains, a bartender informs us, use wastewater recycled from guests' rooms. Despite his admonitions and fervent offers of bottled designer water, we down tap water by the gallons, never slaking our thirst. The bartender knows where his water comes from: Lake Mead, he says. We slug it down. Chlorine Lite with a bouquet of Evinrude.

In Las Vegas, the best survival strategy is a wholesale reduction of Self to imbecilic dipstick, easily managed in these clockless, windowless mazes of flashing lights and blaring gaming devices with nary a molecule of The Environment allowed across the transom. The idea is complete disconnection from Earth, a realignment of the senses through a techno-collage of myths and fantasies conjured by corporate hacks. At the Tropicana, I inspect each potted palm for signs of life. Then we transfer to the Río, Where It Is Always Carnival and not much different from the other casinos save for the Brazilian motif and the tiny televisions mounted above each video poker machine. I peer into the foliage of potted banana trees, expecting at least a cricket. No palm, no leaf, no pot is real, only the cigarette butts.

Mark disappears, mumbling about the anthropology of dentalfloss bikinis and a stripper named Bunny Fajitas. Before I'm trampled to death by a shriek of Rotarians from Pocatello, I duck away to rest on an outskirt, unused stair step. From there I watch a terrified woman in bright native African dress clutch the rail of a descending escalator in a death grip. At the escalator's foot, her family nurses her down in their melodic native tongue — from Senegal, perhaps, evidently an escalatorless nation. She survives. Everyone hugs. Hoover Dam's turbines juice the guitars and keyboards of a live band in the lobby. Smurf Intellect, Los Deli Meats, Heavy Trim Beef Primals, I didn't catch the name but the lyrics concern whips. A man in a crisp white shirt and dark slacks (waiter? missionary?) tells me I cannot sit on this step. I cannot sit anywhere, he asserts officiously, except on the stools at bars, poker and slot machines, and blackjack tables. He stares down his nose at me as if I had dripped cobra spit on his shoes and barks, "You must leave." Where's the river? Take me to the river. Take me to Senegal. At the Excalibur no one can be persuaded to induce hydro-gridlock by a simultaneous political flush of their toilets. Water simply seems too bounteous; it fills hoses, sprinklers, fountains, waterfalls, water slides, swimming pools, wishing wells, moats, fish tanks, and artificial lakes; it greens an epidemic of golf courses and chills a million cocktails.

A grown man in scarlet doublet and mustard yellow panty hose plops a tinsel wreath on my head and recites a sonnet in bad high-school Chaucer, prologue to a halfhearted sell on tickets to a jousting tournament. Somehow he knows I'm not the jousting type, but he lets me keep the wreath. A woman standing next to a video poker machine catches my eye: Liv Ullmann face, shorts, running shoes, a thick blond braid down her back, a dippy smile across a tanned face. She is singing from *The Sound of Music*. In strikingly muscular arms she clutches a grocery bag filled with folded newspapers. She rivets her gaze on the video machine as if it were Christopher Plummer or an Alp and belts out, "The hills are alive…"

Daft with the sheer profusion of man-made matter, Mark and I return to our hotel room and fling ourselves onto the bed, hot, weighty sheets draped over our fantasy-stuffed bodies, our feet protruding like Jesus' under the shroud in Mantegna's painting *The Lamentation Over the Dead Christ*. Sometime in the fitful night, a voice crackles over the intercom box above the bathroom doorway. "Please do not panic," the voice urges us. "The fire alarms mean nothing. Please stay in your rooms."

The river of traffic streaming down the Strip will kill me if I back up three feet off the boulevard curb, where I'm in the bushes risking my life to study nature in Vegas's endangered vacant lots, its postage-stamp plots of unpaved Mojave. The inventory so far: crickets, ants, pigeons, wind-strewn "escort girl" flyers as numerous as scutes on a pit viper, and a playing card (the king of spades). Cowbirds (those toxic parents!) chase kazooing cicadas through muffler-sizzled oleander bushes too spindly in foliage to hide the random upturned shopping cart or shade me from sunlight intensified by its infinite reflection off chrome and windshields. I observe one stunted specimen of Aleppo pine, *Pinus halepensis*, a drought-tolerant Mediterranean import largely relegated to freeways and residential areas. I find few bugs in the bush and plenty in the yellow pages under "Pests": termites, earwigs, roaches, pill bugs, silverfish, scorpions, plus rodents and a category called "olive control." Physiographically the Mojave Desert is a transitional province between the Great Basin to the north and the Sonoran Desert to the south. Biological boundaries of all three deserts mix here, so one would expect creosote bush, catclaw, mesquite, yucca, geckos, horned lizards, and the like. But hardly a particle of native flora or fauna lives in Strip habitat. I crawl out of the bushes and hike to safety. Off to find the meadows, *las vegas*.

Negligible rainfall, barely four inches annually, comes to the austere bowl of desert in which Las Vegas spreads. Over a century and a half ago, a carpet of spring-fed grasslands grew in this basin, an oasis in a sea of thorns, alkali, and dust. Except for an occasional flash flood through the washes, the nearby mountains flushed little moisture from their peaks. The basin's water came from an underground aquifer created during the Pleistocene, when rainfall was abundant. Big Springs surfaced in a mad gurgle to form the headwaters of Las Vegas Creek, which flowed easterly along the valley floor, then disappeared into the sand. An exploration party in 1844 recorded the creek's temperature at 115 degrees. Eleven years later a Mormon mission watered travelers between Salt Lake City and California settlements. The missionaries also mined lead from an ore vein along the nearby Colorado River and shipped it north to be made into bullets by the church's public works unit. The missionaries took it upon themselves — these were busy people — to teach the Indians, mostly Paiute, "farming and hygiene," although no one bothered to ask the Indians if they cared to farm or needed help in attending to their bodies. Nineteenth-century zealotry seemed obsessed with putting natives behind plows, in pants. "Discontent with the teepee and the Indian camp," claimed Merrill Gates of the U.S. Board of Indian Commissioners in the 1880s, "is needed to get the

Indian out of the blanket and into trousers — and trousers with a pocket in them, and with a pocket that aches to be filled with dollars!"

By 1907 wells tapped much of the groundwater. Their strength — good water at constant pressure — and cheap land lured more settlers, who drained the meadows for crops and pasture. For nearly fifty years water flowed into farm, pipe, and oblivion; no one capped the wells until 1955. Las Vegas Creek had dried up five years before. Big Springs, now under pavement and the lock and key of the municipal water district, surfaced no more, and parts of the Las Vegas Valley had subsided as much as five feet, so much water had been mined. The meadows disappeared but for a trace, I was told, at Lions Club and Fantasy Park near downtown Las Vegas.

I drive to Fantasy Park on a boulevard that parallels a brief stretch of creek straitjacketed by concrete riprap. The creek begins and ends in enormous culverts; it merely belches aboveground for a few blocks so people can throw their litter into it. Fantasy Park grows limp-leafed trees in even rows, and despite a posting that the park is for children twelve and under, a few prostrate bodies of napping transients drop bombs of drool into a rather seedy lawn. Casino blitz envelops the park, buffered by mortuaries. Downtown Las Vegas, once heartland of the economy of sin, is now an outlier to the upscale Strip. Unless razed, it has no space for the entertainment mall, the computer-programmed volcano, artificial rain forest, concourse of Roman statuary, circus, castle, or thirty-story pyramid.

However outstripped by the illusion vendors of the nineties, surely downtown Las Vegas scores highest for the Stupidity of Man exhibit's best archival photograph. The 1951 photograph shows Vegas Vic, a landmark, sixty-foot-high neon cowboy on the cornice of the Pioneer Club, beckoning the pilgrims to girls, gambling, and glitz. His thumb is up, his cigarette dangles from his lips. Behind Vegas Vic and the cityscape rises a white-hot cloud on a slender stem, one of the atom wranglers' earliest nuclear bombs, popped off on ground zero less than a hundred miles away.

In Fantasy Park the homeless nappers awaken and roll off what would be the meadows' last stand had a lawn not replaced them. One of the men zombie-walks across the turf to the Binary Plasma Center. Two others approach me for spare change, grass clippings stuck to their sweaty T-shirts. I donate my Fun Book, a collection of courtesy coupons for drinks, playing chips, and discounts at beauty parlors. Casually I ask them where Las Vegas water comes from. The answer is unanimous: the faucet.

Las Vegas's faucets feed one of the highest per-capita water consumption rates in the nation, serving over 800,000 residents, twenty million visitors a year, and a monthly influx of several thousand new residents, most of them quality-of-life refugees from California. To feed the housing boom and the gaming industry's insatiable quest for the next great attraction, Las Vegas will likely be using every last drop of its legal share of Colorado River by the year 2002. It has considered buying water from a desalination plant in Santa Barbara, California, to trade with Los Angeles for rights to more Colorado River water. Las Vegas secured the last of the unappropriated groundwater in its own valley and seeks unclaimed water from the nearby Virgin River. It has also applied to import water from aquifers beneath the "empty" basins in Nevada's outback — fossil water, the ancient rain stored since the Pleistocene and rationed to the surface in spring creeks and seeps that give life to bighorn sheep, fish, lizards, plants, birds, and ranchers. The controversy pits rural Nevada against Las Vegas, sparking memories of a water grab by another lifestyle-obsessed megalopolis: the plumbing of eastern Sierra Nevada runoff by the city of Los Angeles during the early century, an exportation that drained the Owens Valley nearly dry. Sierra water, stored in snowpack, renews itself. Nevada's aquifers would be mined.

While everyone tries to predict the nature of a twenty-first century water war, thousands more newcomers unpack and scream for faucets. Unless a tarantula leaps up and bites off their lips, few seem to notice they live in a desert. At the Las Vegas Natural History Museum, my next research stop, the feature exhibit is a three-hundred-gallon tank swarming with those fascinating Mojave Desert endemics: live sharks.

What does it take to make this emphatically arid place livable? Shade and water. The endless ripple of malls, warehouses, manufacturing plants, minicasinos, restaurants, car dealers, trailer parks, and spanking new residential estates beyond Strip and city speak of a desert culture carried leagues beyond those amenities by a titanic appetite. America's deserts became habitable by virtue of artifice, the replacement of natural flora, a rearrangement of contours, and most significant, the realignment of water: tap the springs and creeks, recontour the basin and flats, harness massive quantities of power and water from a river that flows through the chocolate brown andesite breccia walls of a primeval canyon that in the process is obliterated. We are on our way to Hoover Dam.

The basin cants away from the city toward the rough jumble of peaks above the Colorado River and Hoover's reservoir, Lake Mead. Someone has unpacked platter after platter of hundred-acre subdivisions, repeated motifs of flamingo pink and turquoise stucco with red, Spanish-style tile roofs. Concrete lining reroutes washes and arroyos to take the summer's flash floods somewhere, elsewhere. Hefty stucco walls enclose each community, deterring entry by thieves, perverts, Gila monsters, and lawn-spoiling Russian olive trees. The self-contained suburbs boast names like Legacy Legends and Verde Viejo. Who could lure real-estate dollars to places with names like Hell's Skillet, Arsenic Springs, Donkey Butt Wash, Limp Dick Crick?

The morning sizzles at ninety-six degrees before eight o'clock. Close to the dam, cars creep bumper to bumper beneath the giant towers and webs of transmission lines that carry rivers of energy to Nevada, California, and Arizona. We park short of the dam and join the queue under a skimpy aluminum ramada to await a shuttle bus that takes tourists the last few miles to the dam's crest. A sign reads WATCH FOR BIGHORN SHEEP, but everyone watches for the shuttle, deep-roasted outside their air-conditioned vehicles, red ants gnawing their ankles. Desolation Canyon has accustomed Mark and me to such discomfort, although we cannot assume a relaxed Fremont squat on the ground because it is covered in broken glass. For an hour we stand like stoic Kalahari hosts among rather testy Eskimo guests.

Several years ago I shed mud-caked river shoes and rude shorts, dressed respectably, and walked into the visitor center of another Colorado River megadam. Politely I asked the receptionist, "What would this river look like without the dam?" (Should I have flung my participles about so carelessly? Used *did* instead of *would*? Was Dr. Freud in the room?) The receptionist looked at me as if I had just stuffed angry sharks into his pants. "Excuse me for a moment," he rasped, and disappeared behind an office door. The floor vibrated quietly as turbines somewhere in the dam's bowels mangled their requisite five hundred cats a minute. These dams unnerve me, they push encephalitic fluids against my skull, they hair up my tongue as though I had been licking lightbulb filaments. I felt the River's pressure, the lurking power of the outlaw. Before the receptionist returned I had to leave.

Today, at Hoover Dam, I have promised Mark I shall be on my best behavior. Alas, as the humming voltaics lop three years off our life spans, the courage I conjured to haul myself into the innards of Hoover suddenly fails, research be damned. We flee back to the truck and drive across the dam.

The angular rock of Black Canyon tilts, coils, and juts in colors that range from dark brown to purplish black. A construction road cut exposes a bright pink interior, a rock version of a yawning hippopotamus. No one spoke up for a wild Black Canyon, no moss-backed biocentric heretics suggested that humanity view nature as a mother rather than a pet or slave. In the thirties everyone was speaking up for jobs and relief from the Depression.

Gridlock stalls us on the dam's crest, where shuttles disgorge tourists who line up to buy tickets to make the descent into the powerhouse. "People still come here, drawn by the spirit of the Colorado," a tour brochure proclaims. I desperately seek river spirit to the left of the dam crest — a hundred miles upcanyon across Lake Mead, amidst Jet Skis, Wave Runners, houseboats, fluorescent jet boats, and a fifty-foot bathtub ring — and to its right — the undrowned canyon squirting a limpid stream from the dam's foot. Nearly a quarter mile below the rims of Black Canyon, the Río Colorado runs cold and clear, bereft of its red-brown complexion, its silt and peculiar native fish. It is neither *río* nor *colorado* but a thin, blue-green lake slackened by Lake Mohave, the reservoir behind the next dam sixty-seven miles downstream, another stair step in the plumbing that extends the remainder of the Colorado's course to the dry sands of Mexico.

We U-turn on the Arizona flank of the dam and cross back over the crest, ensnared in a second gridlock. My father, who watched Los Angeles boom and bloom on Colorado River water and hydropower as he grew up in the twenties and thirties, remembers that Boulder Dam, as

Hoover Dam was first named, put men to work, four thousand Depression-starved men who desperately needed work, and food on the table of hungry families. Between 1931 and 1935, dam workers poured three and a quarter million cubic yards of concrete into this chasm with hardly a sandbar or ledge for footing and the indefatigable river roaring through the bypass tunnels, exposing the Mesozoic bedrock and ooze of a watercourse 13 million years in the making. I peer over Hoover's lip and think of the workers who fell to their deaths during construction. Legend says they still lie buried in the dam they built, limbs outstretched in descent now ossified in concrete. The dam was not poured in a solid mass. Solid, it would have dried 125 years later. Workers constructed a 726.4-foot-high stack of house-sized forms, two hundred hollow wooden boxes filled with concrete cooled by refrigerant piped through copper tubing, forms now hidden under the smooth, arching sheath of concrete athwart the dark walls of Black Canyon. Under construction, Hoover Dam looked like Swiss cheese.

We drive by the transmission towers for a final dose of electromagnetic radiation. Lake Mead spreads to the northeast, saved from suffocation by Glen Canyon Dam upstream. Glen trapped the millions of tons of sediment that were filling Lake Mead at an alarming rate soon after Hoover Dam was built, threatening to render Hoover useless in about a hundred years. Lake Powell and its arms up Cataract Canyon and the Dirty Devil, San Juan, and other tributary rivers now hold the sediment behind Glen Canyon Dam. With Glen, the Colorado River's delta has moved from the Gulf of California to Nevada and Utah.

Hoover Dam rid the "natural menace," as the Bureau of Reclamation calls the virgin Colorado River, of its mud and its fury. During our tenure in the West, before the dam and since, we have loved neither mud nor fury. We have never loved this river. We have made war on it as if it were a pack of proud, unruly, elusive Apaches. Chase them down, catch them, tame them. Put pants on them. Hoover, Glen, and the others, triumphs in the reduction of wild river to tool, stand as secular cathedrals to environmental mastery, the monolithic beads in the necklace of river from Wyoming to Mexico, monuments to our species' uncanny ability to know how to do things and our failure to ask whether the environmental consequences might simply be too great.

Las Vegas makes no bones about its premier commodity — honest fraud — but I don't care much for the place. The exceptions, however, are the pink tongues on the pudgy white tigers in their all-white neo-Babylonian habitat box on the entry concourse of the Mirage Hotel and Casino. Each time I visit the tigers, they sleep behind their plate-glass shield, their languid, potbellied bodies sprawled across elevated benches, the sweet tongues drowsily lolling below exquisitely whiskered cheeks. The Mirage sucks a river of people off the Strip onto its moving sidewalks, channels them past the narcoleptic cats and a wall-sized aquarium of parrot fish, wrasses, angelfish, sharks, and other tropical prisoners, and spills them into the tributaries that flow to gaming rooms, bars, shops, and restaurants. Earlier I had seen the Sound of Music woman sleeping on a patch of Strip lawn, a bag lady with one grocery bag and the body of a marathon runner. Now she is here, singing to the poker machines, and I would gleefully join her had I not the singing voice of gargled bats. Like mobile tide pools, a shoal of Frenchmen in bright aloha shirts riffles noisily forward with the stream. Perched on bar stools like herons on a riverbank are Vegas's sunset women, hard-fleshed, sinewy women in crayon makeup, pink stilettos, and gazes to convince the most egocentric lout that they know far more than he does. These women should be allowed to run Las Vegas. They probably do.

In the bar beneath the Mirage's artificial rain forest, Mark sips a herbivore's daiquiri afloat with Chinese parasols, fruit, carrots, celery, and other verdure. He scouts for naysaying casino personnel while I dive under the table and crawl around the rain forest in search of wildlife. The thicket grows bromeliads, ferns, philodendrons, cricket noises, and roof-raking palm trees that thrust fat boles up through the epoxied floor. The philodendrons are real. I emerge, harvest the crop from my daiquiri, and study the couple across from us, whose furtive looks reveal that some outlaw love may soon be consummated.

Our cocktail server, who thinks her water comes from California but is not sure, enlightens us about the construction crews that were furiously ingesting the Strip's remnant open spaces. We had seen the activity earlier in the day, and we wondered about the new building in the parking lot behind the Circus Circus Casino.

"What are they building at Circus Circus?" Mark asks.

"That's the Grand Slam Canyon," she tells us, clearing the table of peach pits, orange rinds, celery leaves, kelp.

Grand Slam Canyon promises the Grand Canyon without the Grand Canyon's pesky discomforts — its infernal heat, wind, roadlessness, and size that defies the three-day vacation, its cacti, lizards, snakes, biting insects, burro poop, boulders, rapids, the possibility of death. Amidst hundred-foot peaks, swimming pools, water slides, pueblos, and a replica of the Grand Canyon's Havasu Falls, inside a climate-controlled, vented, pink womb of a dome, Grand Slam Canyon visitors will fly through rapids and waterfalls in a roller coaster. The River made better than itself.

By midnight my tongue is furry and dry, as if I had swallowed a mouthful of casino carpet. We walk outside the Mirage, where a hundred or more spectators watch a volcano erupt in the palm garden, upstaging a rising moon, spewing fire from propane burners and sloshing wastewater down its tiered slopes. Out from nowhere a single, frantic female mallard duck, her underside lit to molten gold by the tongues of flame, tries desperately to land in the volcano's moat. Mark and I stare incredulously at the duck, two faces pointed skyward among hundreds pointed volcano-ward. Unable to land in this perilous jungle of people, lights, and fire, the duck veers down the block toward Caesars Palace. With a sudden *ffzzt* and a shower of sparks barely distinguishable from the ambient neon, the duck incinerates in the web of transmission lines slicing through a seventy-foot gap in the Strip high-rises, a skein of wire and cable that surges with the power of the River.

Dancing to the Rocky Mountain Quick Step

Ken Olsen

Taping one end of a string to my tongue and swallowing the rest of it — encased in a pill — wasn't my idea of a palatable diagnosis. The thought of the doctor extracting the string after six to twenty-four hours and examining it for microscopic bugs was as objectionable as my five-week bout with diarrhea.

Swallowing and then retrieving a string was the only surefire test for Giardia. Or so the doctor said. Later I would wonder if he was spinning folklore. At that moment, I skipped absolute accuracy and agreed to just take the cure.

When I confronted the mayor of our small southwestern Montana town he readily agreed I had probably contracted Giardia from the public tap. He refused to do anything about it. "I'd have to issue a boil order and that'd panic the town," he pronounced, wedged behind a desk in the tiny city hall office where he convened to hear the complaints of the general public once a week.

"I'm not going to do that. It happened a couple of years ago and it turned out that only seven or eight people caught it."

The political price of telling the townsfolk their water was rife with beaver fever obviously was higher than seven or eight voters suffering the gut-wrecking protozoa. Much less me, editor and publisher of the local weekly newspaper, being afflicted. The mayor even seemed to take pleasure in my illness, undoubtedly believing some of the poison from my pen had seeped into my stomach.

"If your symptoms persist for more than 96 hours, call a physician," my self-help medical guide said. I read it in the bathroom. It's where I spent all of my time before figuring that not eating much of anything sharply decreased my incontinence.

I consumed Pepto Bismol, then switched to Kayopectate. I left my first visit to the doctor sheepishly thinking I had blundered and that changing remedies was the reason for my prolonged "touch of the Rocky Mountain Quick Step," as my mother delicately referred to the malady. The doctor pronounced the switch a mistake. Pepto Bismol, he assured, was the cure for my flu or other passing bug. Kayopectate was not right for my problem, he said.

And there was no hint, in that second week, of a water-borne culprit. There was no hint that one of the most common human parasites was at home in my small intestine.

My lips soon bore a faint, dried-pink ring, evidence of my chugging the over-the-counter remedy. I'd dispensed with a spoon. Too slow for the doses I required.

The self-help book — a gift from the company health-insurance carrier — prescribed the BRAT diet: bananas, rice, applesauce, and toast. BRAT is no match for Giardia.

My partner whipped up Jello and bullion and searched for ways to tame the serpent in my innards. My mother scrutinized my condition by phone, from a thousand miles away, sharing every home remedy she remembered.

Father diagnosed stress.

Five or six months before, on my 30th birthday, I'd arrived in the Beaverhead Valley to fire the news staff and supposedly retake control of the weekly newspaper owned by the small family corporation I worked for. The company president swore the paper was in the black and only needed a little steady guidance to mint money. My ego took the bait.

Once a daily, the newspaper had shriveled to a weekly as the town, agriculture, the railroad, gold mining, and everything else shriveled. The bank account also had somehow shriveled by the time we arrived. "In the black" turned out to be tens of thousands of dollars in the red. Checks for a year's worth of bills were neatly written, signed, and clipped to the front of the checkbook, awaiting the imaginary day when the paper could afford to cover them and they could be mailed.

The newspaper lived day-to-day in a decrepit two-story brick building with a cadaverous basement that fit its rumored legacy as the former town morgue. Plastic sheeting caught rain and snowmelt that came through the roof and funneled it out the back windows upstairs. I became well acquainted with the woman from the power company who constantly called to threaten shutting off the heat because of the lack of payment.

My partner also worked in this dive, one of the bonuses offered if we took the job. She and another reporter tried to pry stories out of a tight-lipped town angry about the personnel shake up. I tried to collect money from advertising customers — even those with up-to-date accounts — to make payroll or to send to the newsprint company in order to get a few more rolls.

I'd acquired the Florida swampland of positions as a weekly newspaper editor-publisher. My father re-diagnosed stress. I imagined I knew how dysentery-stricken POWs in Vietnam had felt.

Our reporter admired my diet plan and seemed nonplussed by the fact that my pound shedding meant I was always sprinting past her desk to the bathroom. She asked how to get "whatever it is that you have." Somewhere in the midst of all of this, the toilet and the 100-year-old plumbing at the newspaper plugged. I stayed away from the building while it was repaired by the unfortunate pressman. We couldn't afford a plumber.

After consuming bottles of the recommended over-the-counter remedy — chased by handfuls of the same chalky pink stuff in tablet form — I returned to the doctor. He sent me off to a room with sampling cups. I found false hope. The lab found nothing. Later he told me Giardia isn't easily detected by such routine samples.

Well into the fourth week, the doctor decided to try something stronger, something prescription. Shock waves continued coursing through my stomach. Jello was a sentence, not a meal. But it seemed to affect me the least, and had a chance of fooling my body into thinking I was attempting to do something about hunger.

I started calling the doctor almost daily. That prompted him to go out on a limb, nearly five weeks after my first dance to the Quick Step, and give me the cure for Giardia without the string test. Within a few days, I was a whole person. Luckily. The drug of choice for Giardia — quinacrine — apparently can cause nausea, vomiting, and turn your skin yellow. I have no idea if that's the wonder drug that nuked my pet parasite, nor any desire to know. Contemplating it makes me queasy.

Giardia. Once the doctor said it, I knew right where I'd contracted the parasites, the water I had drunk and the restaurant where I'd downed them. As a backpacker, I also knew it wasn't likely the eatery's fault. It was the town drinking water pond: a reservoir fed by creeks that were open to any animal that could do anything it wanted in them, like spread Giardia. I belatedly remembered rumors of problems with the town reservoir.

How cruel, I thought. In my trips to the back country, I always take the most prophylactic approach to safe drinking. Anyone with any time on the trails knows you can't stick your face in a cold, clear mountain stream and drink with impunity. Except for my partner, who can consume gallons from the filthiest puddle and go untouched. But even she danced a bit to the Giardia fiddler when I was stricken.

When backpacking, we'd cook water forever to get it to the required boiling for a duration of "one minute for every thousand feet of elevation." When the backpacking stove ran out of fuel, that meant a fire, which meant charcoal- and ash-laden water. Gatorade it was not. A draught of this warm brew on a dusty trail parched more than it quenched. That led to the purchase of an expensive, Swiss-made filter-clad water pump. Charcoal-ade, lugging a pump; anything beat the stories we'd heard of Giardia.

Giardia. Or Giardiasis, as it's called once it's making itself known to your body. Along with Cryptosporidia, Giardia turned up in 97 percent of recent tests of United States and Canadian water, according to the National Resources Defense Council. The water was tested before it was treated for drinking. But treatment is no comfort since faulty purification systems are a major culprit in Giardia and Cryptosporidia outbreaks. Most of the nation's large water utilities use pre-World War I technology which isn't up to removing most dangerous contaminants, the NRDC says.

Though it was discovered in the late 1600s by a scientist experiencing diarrhea, Giardia was thought innocuous for a long time. Now it's recognized as an important problem in developing countries, and often the first intestinal pathogen to affect children, according to Dr. Stephen Martin, an assistant professor of medicine at the University of Cincinnati.

Giardia probably became noticed as a health threat when a Colorado ski-town chamber of commerce discovered it was an economic threat. The first major outbreak in the United States was reported in Aspen in 1965, when one hundred twenty-three skiers were laid low.

Few city dwellers realize an estimated 50 million Americans drink poorly treated water, laced with everything from tetrachloroethylene to protozoa and parasites. Except maybe 3,800 residents of Pittsfield, Massachusetts, who contracted Giardia from their local water supply nine years ago.

An average of 4 percent of the people in the United States get Giardia, and that number hits 16 percent in some of the more mountainous regions. However, not everybody with Giardia contracts chronic diarrhea.

Giardia. As I mentioned, I alerted the mayor to this important public health issue.

We had never bonded, the mayor and I. If he hadn't chosen the anti-Ken Olsen camp the day I arrived in town and naïvely fired it's favorite reporter-photographer on orders from headquarters, he joined within a month. The mayor, like lots of locals, took affront early on when I unleashed an editorial criticizing a proposal to use taxpayers money to revive the local college football team. Montana couldn't afford to support six public college football programs I reasoned. If the alumni wanted Frontier Conference bruisers chasing a pigskin, let them pony up the money.

I'd overlooked the link between sports and patriotism. Town residents lined up at my door to deliver letters to the editor. As words went, they were armor piercing.

When the mayor passed off my Giardia complaint like I was the queen of spades in a hearts game, I retreated. I was too embarrassed to make an issue of it. I didn't want local folk to have any hint of my misery they could take glee in. Medication had obviously dulled my senses if I thought that a town that small had kept the secret of my diagnosis, much less my wholesale purchase and consumption of bullion, Jello, and Pepto Bismol. The mayor, obviously afraid of the reaction, never raised the issue again either.

Though they had not helped, I ate Rice Krispies and other BRAT food for months afterwards as if it was necessary to keep from upsetting the unseen but powerful spirit in my stomach. I winced when I thought of string pills and never left home without some over-the-counter cure. Though it dealt with the opposite of my problem, I had a greater appreciation for television commercials describing regularity remedies for elderly people. I knew the handicap of a dysfunctional system.

For years, I drank only bottled water, hauling gallons of it from the grocery store. In summer, it meant a water run most every night. I spent thousands of dollars on those plastic jugs, but I spent no time doing the Rocky Mountain Quick Step. I still think of the glass of water that comes with the menu as potential misery, not common courtesy. I regard the glass, brushing condensation from the sides, and wonder whether the parasite that, in its active form looks like a bearded man, swims within.

The mayor and I collided again over another public health threat — a cop who drank too much and chased unwilling women. I had enough calluses by then that I didn't care. I didn't back down. Perhaps the mayor, by way of Giardia, had helped me find the intestinal fortitude I needed.

Photographs

@@@

Aaron Johanson

He almost got the better of me, that Japanese third-grader.

"Tell me the name of Japan's largest island!" he demanded of me with his 100-decibel voice. By emphasizing the word *island*, my little interrogator hoped to distract me from the correct answer, Honshu, which translates as "main island," and is the center of Japan's government, business, and industry. So prominent is it, in fact, that even Japanese people forget that it is also one of the nation's 6,852 islands.

Having been through third grade myself, an American one (centuries ago), I saw through his trick. To his dismay, I added to the above that Hokkaido ranks as Japan's second largest island and is bordered by the Japan Sea, Okhotsk Sea, Pacific Ocean, two channels, numerous bays, and harbors.

I spent three years living in, and photographing the farthest (and, I suppose, the nearest) reaches of the island — an area just over half the size of Oregon. In addition to being surrounded by water, Hokkaido has several of Japan's largest lakes.

So, I shot a lot of water in my travels. I used double exposures because they seem to convey the way water physically and psychologically flows through the lives of Hokkaido's island residents. I like the way double exposures can "fuse" disparate times and places. For me, they express the fluidity and omnipresence of water better than single-exposure photographs.

I mostly used a square image, medium-format camera with interchangeable film magazines. "River suite" was taken near the mouth of the Columbia River, the other images presented here were taken on Japan's second largest island. On occasion, considerable time elapsed between the initial and subsequent exposure that make up each photograph. In my exposure data, I refer to this interval as Total Elapsed Time, or TET.

The long, wrong road
(TET: *2 hours*)

Dreams in silent seas
(TET: *1 minute*)

River suite
(TET: *1 hour*)

Aquatic spotlight
(TET: *5 minutes*)

Lunch hour ablution
(TET: *5 minutes*)

And this is why I sojourn here
(TET: *2 days*)

Falls and the scaffold of Babel
(TET: *1 minute*)

Drop

ᛇ

Nancy Lord

Some summers the creek at my Alaskan fish camp runs high and some summers low. This dry season I've had to make frequent trips up the creek to adjust a network of pipes and hoses that funnel water into a weighted wooden barrel, the start of our gravity-fed water system.

This day, as I reposition a hose in a rock-dammed pool, a dark cloud in the mottled sky spits rain that patterns the rocks with solid round dots. I think of the same cloud passing inland and unloading drops to bounce against the surface of the lake before mixing into the water that will later find its way down this creek. I rarely contemplate water in any of its forms without conjuring up a schoolbook illustration showing the cycle of evaporation, clouds, rain, and water running to the sea, with various side trips through the roots of trees or storage as glacial ice. The wonder of this, as with so much in nature, has never left me.

Rain spatters on my head, and I indulge myself in a conceit, imagining a single drop falling into the lake. I imagine it does not evaporate back into cloud, is not absorbed by the surrounding land and thirsty roots, but one day — still holding to its dropular form — rides up against the beaver dam at the lake's end. It slips through, part of a melodious trickle between alder sticks and packed mud into a shallow, weed-filed creek. For a time, the drop circles in an eddy behind a marsh marigold root, then is caught in the push of other drops from behind. Moving into the sluggish current, it bounces like a slow-motion pinball from bank to bank, rising as it warms in a sunny pool, sinking again as other, warmer drops flow over it. The drop works its way over smooth stones, past the treading action of thousands of mosquito larvae. It escapes the thirst of a varied thrush that stops its drink long enough to sing a burry note. Running quickly through a narrow course, it disappears under an overhang of turf only to swirl back and get carried along once again, past alder thickets, around stands of prickly devil's club, under fallen spruce. It floats into a glassy pond and then through another dam, around a second pond and over a spillway, into a more meandering creek. Rubbing over stones past an aphid flailing on its back, the drop finally falls over the bluff's lip into sunlight and starts its faster run down the draw.

In a leap through time, I imagine this chimerical drop slithering over algae, bumping one more boulder, becoming part of the gurgling I hear up ahead, coming my way over gravel and flakes of coal. It heads pell-mell into a tunnel of smooth black pipe and free falls into a frothy mix of water and air held within the woody, slick barrel sides. It smacks a rock in the barrel's bottom, then rises with the rest of the water toward overflow at the barrel's rim. On the way to the rim, the drop is sucked into another pipe, this one a narrow black hose. For the next eight hundred feet it zips through the pitch dark stream by way of a series of narrower couplings, down, down, finally into a narrower green hose that spurts at last through a spray nozzle into a large tub.

This is our hot tub, a cattle watering trough, hard black plastic, the Rubbermaid name emblazoned on the side. It sits on our deck at the edge of the sea and is suitably comfortable for two friendly people who will recline with backs to curved ends and chins at water level. My fanciful water drop has beat me down the hill to be part of a tub filling. Ken is making a fire under copper coils, turning the pump to its lowest speed. The cold drop sinks, leaves the tub through yet another hose, passes through pump and hot coils, returns to the tub, one hot drop.

And here I am. I don't wait for the tub to steam, as I do on cold days. The sky has cleared into full sunshine and, although residual storm swells pound the beach, the wind has stilled. As soon as the tub water is bath-water warm, I strip off my clothes and get in. Ken pushes another stick of driftwood into the fire.

The sun, warm on my face, diffuses through the water to light my whole white body. The clear water magnifies, and I suddenly have hips.

Just out from the deck, breakers angle in over the flats, crashing into ribbons of foam. The boat rears and plunges on its mooring. I lie back in the tub, stretched out, floating. The water is silk-smooth against my skin, and I am supremely content. I cannot imagine a finer place in the world, nor a finer moment.

A huge, green-headed moosefly — Alaska's version of a horsefly — lands on the edge of the tub and walks the couple inches down to water level, where it tests the edge of the water with its hairy feelers, like a potential wader checking temperature, then sticks in its tubular mouth and sucks up a stream so urgently it leaves a ripple like a wake. It backs up, turns around, climbs to the rim, cleans its whiskers with a few wipes of its front legs, and flies off. I think that must be the warmest water it's ever had reason to sip, although the females of their kind feed on blood, delivering the nastiest insect bites known in these parts.

The water heats up. I make room for Ken. Displaced water overflows the tub and splashes to the deck, drains to the sand. Underwater surges bounce between ends of the tub. I am up to my ears, and all the muscles of my back turn loose and ropy.

Beside us, three white totes, scavenged at sea to use for net storage, take up most of the space on the deck. They are four-foot square and nearly as deep, with lids, and on top of the lids are set smaller totes — the red and gray ones we use for hauling and brining fish, for doing laundry, and mixing cement. There's a hunk of scavenged plywood, with rounded corners, we use as a fish cleaning table. There's a huge piece of ball-and-socket hardware Ken had made to attach a boom to our latest flagpole. The pole itself lies flat beside the deck and back along the creek, a victim of storm tides; its enormous root end — a cluster of big rocks and cement around the tarred wood base — now offers a way of climbing to the far side of the deck and gives us something sturdy to tie our running line to. Also on the deck with us is a bent cooking pot with a bar of sandy soap and a shampoo jar that's inside a plastic bag because its lid was reassigned to a gas can. An old net lies in a lump off my end of the tub, partially covered with a blue tarp, some of its corks dangling over the edge. A five-gallon bucket, a piece of fishy burlap, a scrub brush, the end of a pole that fell on the deck when an earlier boom pole collapsed — these are the familiar things that share our immediate area, the stuff of our fishing lives.

I soak and gaze fondly upon all this, a kingdom of sorts, not the cluttered mess another person might think it — no, not at all — but each of it an element of our lives, a necessary part, a story. I need only to look a few feet past the deck to see Ken's stainless steel sink, a set of rusted bedsprings that makes part of our breakwater, our old decrepit cart, the cabin with its own surrounding of important parts. John McPhee wrote in his classic book and Alaska, *Coming into the Country*, that those places you pass on back roads in various parts of the United States, with old car parts and washing machines piled in the yard, belong to Alaskans who just haven't left yet. It's true that in Alaska, in remote areas, and particularly at working places like mining claims or fish camps, it's unwise to get rid of something you will likely need, at least in part, at a later date. Deflated buoys, scraps of line, an empty mayonnaise jar — you will need these things. You will treasure the splintered square of plywood, the foot-length piece of hose, the handle of a wheelbarrow even older than the cart. What you see is not a trashy mess; given the lack of indoor space, each item is actually more or less in its place, waiting for its next use.

Insects seem to be attracted to the heat of the tub, or perhaps I just notice them because I'm bare-skinned and doing nothing except looking. A very tiny dark beetle, not much bigger than a grain of sand, has joined us in the tub, legs flailing. I rescue it and deposit it on the rim. Somehow, though, it's all wrapped up in a drop of water, with most of the droplet under its belly, like an overstuffed beanbag chair it's straddling. It rolls one way and another on the drop, unable to break the surface adhesion. In the sun and on a black surface, the water drop begins almost immediately to shrink. The beetle tilts lower and lower like a car being brought down by a jack. Then the water's gone, and the beetle hangs out its double wings to dry, reminding me of the way cormorants also spread their wings to dry in the sun. I look away, and when I look back the beetle is gone.

I hold my hand in front of my face and look through the water drops that swell and dangle on the ends of my fingers. I locate a view of my opposite arm and regard the shimmer of skin color, then find a wooden post and do the same thing. I look through a drop at Ken, bringing my hand closer to my face and then farther away, until I capture him most completely, upside down and backwards, refracted. The outline of the droplet forms a silver-edged frame. I look for the skiff on the mooring but can't find it through my mirror, can't figure the distortions and angles to bring it into my sight from such a distance. I only find a deep, deep blue, bluer than either sky or water, a concentrate of color, as though the drop sucks color into itself. Each drop is a lens, a magnifier, a jewel. They fall, one by one from my fingertips, and I dip another handful of riches.

The tub water gets too hot, and we stand in the breeze to cool ourselves. We turn on the cold-water hose and aim it at the top of our heads, watch the blood fill each other's faces. We leave the hose in the tub and let it massage us like a Jacuzzi jet. When the sun begins to flicker behind the alders and we feel as though our bones have turned to cooked pasta, we stir ourselves to fill and hang the shower bag, then wash and shampoo on the deck.

I think again of the one drop of water that might have fallen as rain and come down the creek and pipeline to our tub. Where is it now? It might have been swallowed by the moosefly or evaporated from under the tiny beetle. It might have overflowed the tub or served as one of my lenses on the world. I imagine it, though, inside the shower bag and now streaming down over my hair and my hot soapy shoulders, now falling to the sand and draining to the edge of the sea, now being taken back by the next wave.

Flowing

Gary Snyder

Headwaters

Hot head doused under the bronze
      dragon-mouth jet of cold water
      from a cliffside spring —
      at the headwaters
      of the Kamo River north of Kyoto
      Shrine of the Cliff-wall Fudo
Blue-faced growling Fudo,

Lord of the Headwaters, makes
Rocks out of water,
Water of rocks

•

Riverbed

Down at the riverbed
      singing a little tune.
      tin cans, fork stick stuck up straight,
      half the stones of an old black campfire ring,

The monkey dancers, rags and tatters
      wives all whores,
      and the children clowns,
      come skipping down
      dance on boulders,
            clever — free —

Gravel scoop bed of the Kamo
> a digger rig set up on truck-bed with
> revolving screen to winnow out the stones
> brushy willow — twists of sand

At Celilo all the Yakima
> Wasco, Wishram, Warmspring people
> catching salmon, talking,
>> napping scattered through the rocks

Long sweep dip-net held by a foam-drenched
braced and leaning man
out on a scaffold rigged and plank stuck over
the whole Columbia River frothing down
he goes   one with the lift and plume
of the water curling
over,

Salmon arching in the standing spray.

•

Falls

Over stone lip
> the creek leaps out as one
> divides in spray and streamers,
> lets it all   go.

Above, back there, the snowfields.
> rocked between granite ribs
> turn spongy in the summer sun
> water slips out under
> mucky shallow flows
> enmeshed with roots of flower and moss and heather
> seeps through swampy meadows
> gathers to shimmer sandy shiney flats
> then soars off ledges —

Crash and thunder on the boulders at the base.
    painless, playing,
    droplets regather
    seek the lowest,
        and keep going down
    in gravelly beds.

There is no use, the water cycle tumbles round —

Sierra Nevada
    could lift the heart so high
    fault block uplift
    thrust of westward slipping crust — one way
    to raise and swing the clouds around —
    thus pine trees leapfrog up on sunlight
    trapped in cells of leaf — nutrient minerals called together
    like a magic song
    to lead a cedar log along, that hopes
        to get to sea at last and be
            a great canoe.

A soft breath, world-wide, of night and day,
    rising, falling,

The Great Mind passes by its own
    fine-honed thoughts,
    going each way

Rainbow hanging steady
    only slightly wavering with the
    swing of the whole spill,
        between the rising and the falling,
        stands still.

I stand drenched in crashing spray and mist,
    and pray.

Rivermouth

Mouth
you thick
vomiting   outward   sighing prairie
    muddy   waters
    gathering all and
    issue it
    end over end
        away. from land.
the faintest grade.
Implacable, heavy, gentle,

— O pressing song.
    liquid butts and nibbles
    between the fingers — in the thigh —
    against the eye

curl round my testicles
drawn crinkled skin
    and lazy swimming cock.

Once sky-clear and tickling through pineseeds
    humus, moss   fern   stone
    but NOW

the vast loosing
    of all that was found, sucked, held
    born, drowned,

sunk sleepily in
to the sea.

    the root of me
    hardens and lifts to you,
    thick flowing river,
    my skin shivers. I quit

    making this poem.

The Lesbian Ocean

Marusya Bociurkiw

The numbing regularity of waves rolling in from the open Pacific hides an important fact: no two waves are identical.
— Rosemary Neering, The Coast of British Columbia

From far across the room I watch *her* moving on the dance floor: confident, graceful, tough, her eyes surveying the room and only occasionally colliding with mine.

I'm dancing with Benita, a friend who dropped out of public view during an obsessively monogamous five-year relationship. Recently dumped, Benita appears at dances again, fish returned to water, trying to re-acclimatize herself to the tides, the habitat, the mating rituals of this corner of the lesbian ocean. Benita surveys the crowd constantly as she dances, her mouth slightly open, her eyes at once feverish and afraid. Intermittently, she throws me coy affectionate glances and plants suggestive little touches on my bum.

Women who have just broken up constantly approach me for advice, sex, or both. Seasoned practitioner of one-night stands that I am, I must seem like a protective shoal to these nervous fishes-out-of-water. But the truth, if they only knew it, is that I'm having monogamy fantasies. And I haven't slept with anyone in over six months. Six months and three days to be exact.

As the song finally ends, I float gently but firmly out of Benita's by now overtly sexual embrace. I need a break from the waves of sexual energy and confusion that roll through the room from all directions. And, I need to strategize around making some kind of connection with *her*.

In the line-up to the washroom, two women in front are engaged in fervent discussion. I move closer.

"I've been thinking about it all week and I'm still not certain what to do. Suzanne says do something, anything, but I just don't know…"

"You've got to do what you think is right. Suzanne will understand, whatever you decide."

"But what if it doesn't work out? She could leave me!"

"Look, honey, it's like anything else. You risk getting wet, but you can pull out at any time."

I'm not exactly sure if they're discussing fist-fucking or a bank heist. Then, as the conversation turns to blue chips, safe investments, and Dow averages, I realize they are working through their personal socio-economic response to the stock market crash.

I stand back and look more carefully. One woman is wearing exquisitely soft leather Danier pants with a designer cowgirl shirt, the other a black raw silk Armani suit. Their outfits combined could pay my rent, my groceries, and my hydro bill for several months. I ponder this question: are these my sisters or does the class war rage on, even in the lesbian ocean?

I decide I need another diversion. The line-up, which is really just a social alternative to the dance floor, is glacially slow. I turn around and watch with shock as she enters the room. She nods perfunctorily to Armani Woman (an ex-lover, perhaps?) and then eyes me appraisingly. I fall into the shivery abyss of her grey-green eyes.

She smiles.

"*Salut*," says my desired one in a deep voice and a Québécois accent.

"Oh. Umm… hi," I gasp and continue to stare.

"Do I know you?" she inquires pleasantly enough, offering me a Gauloise and then lighting it.

"No! I mean, ah, no,…" I gasp, reduced to a coughing mess after a single inhalation of this *très chic* cigarette.

She pats my back jovially.

"Well, you never know. So many dances, so many women…" She

pauses in mid-sentence, as though unsure how the expression ends and shrugs, elegantly.

She turns to chat with someone who has joined the line. I pause to reflect on this outpouring of nouns and qualifiers from the object of my desire, and look bashfully at the floor. The debris of endless community events litters the black and white linoleum: abortion rally leaflets, ticket stubs, Zig Zag rolling papers, and the occasional beer bottle and animal rights petition.

Suddenly, a hand gently touches my hip. I turn reluctantly, anticipating an ever-more-persistent Benita, but it's *her*, smiling.

"*Voilà*, I think the toilet is free."

Like Persephone fleeing Hades, I sprint into the cubicle, relieved to be liberated from the amused scrutiny of my lusted-after one. I try to think. Contact has occurred sooner than expected and I don't have a plan. Her voice interrupts the chaos of my thoughts.

"Hey, any toilet paper on your side?"

"Oh, yeah, lots, plenty to spare!" I shriek.

"*Parfait...*"

Her hand appears, beckoning, beneath the wall. Slow-motion, I pass over a wad. Slow-motion, her hand lingers against mine and then disappears.

I may have made a lot of mistakes in my life, but there's one thing I know when I see it: flirtation. A cloudy, Vaseline-on-the-lens image of us gliding out of our cubicles and into each other's lives plays itself out on the Cineplex Odeon screen in my head. Tousling my hair, pulling up the collar of my shirt, I swagger out of my booth.

She's gone.

Back on the dance floor, all is as it should be. Couples form and reform, tragedy and romance play themselves out. Women of all shapes and sizes dance, giggle, flirt, or skillfully avoid one another. Beside me, amid great hilarity, the entire Anarcha-Feminist Collective attempts to dance cheek-to-cheek. Nearby, Benita dances, alone, like a bird released from captivity, happy and loose. Beside her are Sumira and Andrea, who met half an hour ago (I introduced them) and are now engaged in what appears to be the act of swallowing each other's mouths. Further away, an ex-lover, Chrystyna, casts sharp, curious glances my way, her head resting on the shoulder of Astarte, another ex-lover (known, at the time, as Sally). I introduced them, too.

But she is nowhere to be seen. *Damn these cavernous Masonic temples,* I think, making my way to where Maya, an old friend from peacenik days, is sitting. Chin in hand, she watches the evermore-furious tides of lesbian energy, with a calm bemused smile. Veteran of about 500 affairs, Maya knows more about the depraved inner goings-on of this community than even the feminist therapists do. If this were the fourth century, Maya would be a soothsayer. If this were a cop show, Maya would be an undercover double-agent. I figure she'll be able to help me.

"Hey, Maya, listen. I need some background on this woman I've been cruising. I don't know her name, but she's francophone, about five-four, short dark hair, slightly femmy…"

"Green eyes?"

"Yeah, amazing green eyes."

Maya mentally searches her all-girl database and pulls up a file.

"Oh, yeah, I know who you mean. Slept with her in…let's see, 1981 or so. Just after the big disarmament rally in New York, you remember the one. I was marching with the Perverts for Peace contingent and she joined in for a while. She had been shopping and was kind of miffed that we had blocked Fifth Avenue. S   yways, I got her stoned at the rally in Central Park and helped her carry her shopping bags home. And the rest, as they say, is herstory…"

"So what's she like?"

"Well, as I recall, she was really nice. Polite, good table manners…"

"Maya."

"…an absolute tiger in bed, likes to wrestle, great lingerie, not very political, but that was, what, ten years ago…Hey, there she is. Hey, she's looking at you!"

And I look back at her. For a moment, we are equals, sexual power meeting its magnetic opposite from either side of the room. Her hands are in her pockets, her hips sway slightly to the music. She looks dreamy or bored, I can't tell which, but she looks at me and I look back. I look and I smile, coyly. I am a predator and this is the jungle. I am Lesbian and this is My Ocean. I am Woman and…

I can't keep it up. I turn to Maya to bum a cigarette.

"Wow," says Maya. Even she is impressed.

I look up again and there she is, again. In a passionate embrace with Armani Woman.

"Oops, I guess she's still with Sandy. They've been together for forever. They own a condo at Harbourfront and play the real estate market, buy up old houses, kick out people who've been living in them for years, and then sell them to rich couples. Sandy comes from old money or something and Suzanne's been a stockbroker for years. It's ironic, really, when you think of the hovels we live in, apt to be evicted at any moment by people like Sandy and Suzanne and here we are, one big happy dyke family. Oh well, live and let live, I always say. But anyways, they're non-monogamous, or so Suzanne tells me, and she's really cute. I say, go for it…"

As Maya launches into her dissertation on the relative merits of non-monogamy, I am saved by Benita, who fairly yanks me onto the dance floor, her eyes ablaze.

"You'll never believe it! I just asked a complete stranger to dance!"

"Did she accept your generous offer?" I manage to ask.

"Well, no. She muttered something about hating Madonna and that she had just come out. So I said to her, 'Look, don't sweat it. After about a year of Top 40 music at women's dances, you'll lose your musical taste buds completely, you'll dance to anything.' Well, it turns out she's, like, an experimental musician, plays with a band called the Dead Virginia Wolves. She said she needed to be alone."

"Oh well, if ya don't cruise, ya lose," I mutter despondently.

"Hey, girlfriend, can't you be a little more supportive? Why only one month ago I was sitting at home on Saturday nights, reading Ikea catalogues with Sarah, discussing vertical blinds and duvet designs, creating complicated pasta sauces, and reading self-help books on Lesbian Bed Death."

I tell her about Suzanne and Sandy, and how differently the stock market crash affects us all. Benita envelops me in a sisterly embrace and we sway to Patsy Cline.

"Hey, girlfriend," she whispers in my ear. "Whaddya say we go back to my pad for some hot… popcorn and a late movie or two?"

Fifteen minutes later we are on the streetcar, passionately debating supply-side economics, love, sex and Madonna, along with Maya, who, stood up by her date, has invited herself along. I sit back for a moment and gaze at their faces, alive with humor and courage: my fellow swimmers heading, momentarily, for the safety of the shore.

Selway

Pam Houston

In the morning the tent was covered all around with a thin layer of ice and we made love like crazy people, the way you do when you think it might be the last time ever, till the sun changed the ice back to dew and got the tent so hot we were sweating. Then Jack got up and made coffee, and we heard the boaters coming just in time to get our clothes on.

They threw us their rope and we caught it. There were three of them, three big men in a boat considerably bigger than ours. Jack poured them coffee. We all sat down on the fallen log.

"You launched late last night?" the tallest, darkest one said. He had curly black hair and a wide open face.

Jack nodded. "Too late," he said. "Twilight boating."

"It's up another half a foot this morning," the man said. "It's supposed to peak today at seven."

The official forest service document declares the Selway unsafe for boating above six feet. Seven feet is off their charts.

"Have you boated this creek at seven?" Jack asked. The man frowned and took a long drink from his cup.

"My name's Harvey," he said, and stuck out his hand. "This is Charlie and Charlie. We're on a training trip." He laughed. "Yahoo."

Charlie and Charlie nodded.

"You know the river," Jack said.

"I've boated the Selway seventy times," he said. "Never at seven feet. It was all the late snow and last week's heat wave. It's a bad combination, but it's boatable. This river's always boatable if you know exactly where to be."

Charlie and Charlie smiled.

"There'll be a lot of holes that there's no way to miss. You got to punch through them."

Jack nodded. I knew Harvey was talking about boat flipping. Big waves that form in holes the river makes behind rocks and ledges and that will suck boats in and hold them there, fill them with water till they flip, hold the bodies, too, indefinitely, until they go under and catch the current, or until the hole decides to spit them out. If you hit a hole with a back wave bigger than your boat perfectly straight, there's a half a chance you'll shoot through. A few degrees off in either direction, and the hole will get you every time.

"We'll be all right in this tank," Harvey said, nodding to his boat, "but I'm not sure I'd run it in a boat that small. I'm not sure I'd run it in a boat I had to bail."

Unlike ours, Harvey's boat was a self-bailer, inflatable tubes around an open metal frame that let the water run right through. They're built for high water, and extremely hard to flip.

"Just the two of you?" Harvey said.

Jack nodded.

"A honeymoon trip. Nice."

"We're not married," Jack said.

"Yeah," Harvey said. He picked up a handful of sand. "The black sand of the Selway," he said. "I carried a bottle of the sand downriver the year I got married. I wanted to throw it at my wife's feet during the ceremony. The minister thought it was pretty strange, but he got over it."

One of the Charlies looked confused.

"Black sand," Harvey said. "You know, black sand, love, marriage, Selway, rivers, life; the whole thing."

I smiled at Jack, but he wouldn't meet my eyes.

"You'll be all right till Moose Creek," Harvey said. "That's when it gets wild. We're gonna camp there tonight, run the bad stretch first thing in the morning in case we wrap or flip or tear something. I hope you won't think I'm insulting you if I ask you to run with us. It'll be safer for us both. The people who flipped yesterday were all experienced. They all knew the Selway.

"They lost one?" Jack said.

"Nobody will say for sure," Harvey said. "But I'd bet on it."

"We'll think about it," Jack said. "It's nice of you to offer."

"I know what you're thinking," Harvey said. "But I've got a kid now. It makes a difference." He pulled a picture out of his wallet. A baby girl, eight or nine months old, crawled across a linoleum floor.

"She's beautiful," I said.

"She knocks me out," Harvey said. "She follows everything with her finger; bugs, flowers, the TV, you know what I mean?"

Jack and I nodded.

"It's your decision," he said. "Maybe we'll see you at Moose Creek."

He stood up, and Charlie and Charlie rose behind him. One coiled the rope while the other pushed off.

Jack poured his third cup of coffee. "Think he's full of shit?" he said.

"I think he knows more than you or I ever will," I said.

"About this river, at least," he said.

"At least," I said.

In midday sunshine, the river looked more fun than terrifying. We launched just before noon, and though there was no time for sightseeing I bailed fast enough to let Jack move the boat through rapids, which came quicker and bigger around every bend. The map showed ten rapids between the put-in and Moose Creek, and it was anybody's guess which of the fifty or sixty rapids we boated that day were the ones the forest service had in mind. Some had bigger waves than others, some narrower passages, but the river was continuous moving white water, and we finally put the map away. On the southern rivers we'd mix rum and fruit juice and eat smoked oysters and pepper cheese. Here, twenty fast miles went by without time to take a picture, to get a drink of water. The Moose Creek pack bridge came into sight, and we pulled in and tied up next to Harvey's boat.

"White fuckin' water," Harvey said." Did you have a good run?"

"No trouble," Jack said.

"Good," Harvey said. "Here's where she starts to kick ass." He motioned with his head downriver. "We'll get up at dawn and scout everything."

"It's early yet," Jack said. "I think we're going on." I looked at Jack's face, and then Harvey's.

"You do what you what," Harvey said. "But you ought to take a look at the next five miles. The runs are obvious once you see them from the bank, but they change at every level."

"We haven't scouted all day," Jack said. I knew he wanted us to run alone, that he thought following Harvey would be cheating somehow, but I believed a man who'd throw sand at his new wife's feet, and I liked a little danger, but I didn't want to die.

"There's only one way through Ladle," Harvey said. "Ladle's where they lost the girl."

"The girl?" Jack said.

"The rest of her party was here when we got here. Their boats were below Ladle. They just took off, all but her husband. He wouldn't leave, and you can't blame him. He was rowing when she got tossed. He let the boat get sideways. He's been wandering around here for two days, I guess, but he wouldn't get back in the boat."

"Jesus Christ," Jack said. He sat down on the bank facing the water.

I looked back into the woods for the woman's husband and tried to imagine a posture for him, tried to imagine an expression for his face. I thought about my Uncle Tim, who spent ten years and a lifetime of savings building his dream home. On the day it was completed he backed his pickup over his four-year-old daughter while she played in the driveway. He sold the house in three days and went completely gray in a week.

"A helicopter landed about an hour ago," Harvey said. "Downstream, where the body must be. It hasn't taken off."

"The water's still rising," Jack said, and we all looked to where we'd pulled the boats up on shore and saw that they were floating. And then we heard the beating of the propeller and saw the helicopter rising out over the river. We saw the hundred feet of cable hanging underneath it and then we saw the women, arched like a dancer over the thick black belt they must use for transplanting wild animals, her long hair dangling, her arms slung back. The pilot flew up the river till he'd gained enough altitude, turned back, and headed over the mountain wall behind our camp.

"They said she smashed her pelvis against a rock and bled to death internally," Harvey said. "They got her out in less then three minutes, and it was too late."

Jack put his arm around my knees. "We'll scout at dawn," he said. "We'll all run this together."

Harvey was up rattling coffeepots before we had time to make love, and I said it would bring us bad luck if we didn't, but Jack said it would be worse than bad luck if we didn't scout the rapids. The scouting trail was well worn. Harvey went first, then Jack, then me and the two Charlies. Double Drop was first, two sets of falls made by water pouring over clusters of house-sized boulders that extended all the way across the river.

"You can sneak the first drop on the extreme right," Harvey said. "There's no sneak for the second. Just keep her straight and punch her through. Don't let her get you sideways."

Little Niagara was a big drop, six feet or more, but the run was pretty smooth and the back wave low enough to break through.

"Piece of cake," Harvey said.

The sun was almost over the canyon wall, and we could hear Ladle long before we rounded the bend. I wasn't prepared for what I saw. One hundred yards of white water stretched from shore to shore and thundered over rocks and logjams and ledges. There were ten holes the size of the one in Double Drop, and there was no space for a boat in between. The currents were so chaotic for such a long stretch there was no way to read which way they'd push a boat. We found some small logs and climbed a rock ledge that hung over the rapid.

"See if you can read this current," Harvey said, and tossed the smallest log into the top of the rapid. The log hit the first hole and went under. It didn't come back up. One of the Charlies giggled.

"Again," Harvey said. This time the log came out of the first hole and survived two more before getting swallowed by the biggest hole, about midway through the rapid.

"I'd avoid that one for sure," Harvey said. "Try to get left of that hole." He threw the rest of the logs in. None of them made it through. "This is big-time," he said.

We all sat on the rock for what must have been an hour. "Seen enough?" Harvey said. "We've still got No Slouch and Miranda Jane."

The men climbed down off the rock, but I wasn't quite ready to leave. I went to the edge of the ledge, lay flat on my stomach, and hung over until my head was so full of the roar of the river I got dizzy and pulled myself back up. The old southern woman said men can't really live unless they face death now and then, and I know by men she didn't mean mankind. And I wondered which rock shattered the dead woman's pelvis, and I wondered what she and I were doing out here on this river when Harvey's wife was home with that beautiful baby and happy. And I knew it was crazy to take a boat through that rapid and I knew I'd do it anyway but I didn't any longer know why. Jack said I had to do it for myself to make it worth anything, and at first I thought I was there because I loved danger, but sitting on the rock I knew I was there because I loved Jack. And maybe I went because his old girlfriends wouldn't, and maybe I went because I wanted him for mine, and maybe it didn't matter at all why I went because doing it for me and doing it for him amounted, finally, to exactly the same thing. And even though I knew in my head there's nothing a man can do that a women can't, I also knew in my heart we can't help doing it for different reasons. And just like a man will never understand exactly how a women feels when she has a baby or an orgasm, or the reasons why she'll fight so hard to be loved, a woman can't know in what way a man satisfies himself, what question he answers for himself, when he looks right at death.

My head was so full of the sound and the light of the river that when I climbed down off the bank side of the ledge I didn't see the elk carcass until I stepped on one of its curled hooves. It was a young elk, probably not dead a year, and still mostly covered with matted brown fur. The skull was picked clean by scavengers, polished white by the sun and grinning. The sound that came out of my mouth scared me as much as the elk had, and I felt silly a few minutes later when Harvey came barreling around the corner followed by Jack.

Harvey saw the elk and smiled.

"It startled me is all," I said.

"Jesus," Jack said. "Stay with us, all right?"

"I never scream," I said. "Hardly ever."

No Slouch and Miranda Jane were impressive rapids, but they were nothing like Ladle and both runnable to the left. On the way back to camp we found wild strawberries, and Jack and I hung back and fed them to each other and I knew he wasn't mad about me screaming. The boats were loaded by ten-thirty and the sun was warm. We wore life jackets and helmets and wet suits. Everybody had diver's boots but me, so I wore my loafers.

"You have three minutes in water this cold," Harvey said. "Even with a wet suit. Three minutes before hypothermia starts, and then you can't swim, and then you just give in to the river."

Harvey gave us the thumbs up sign as the Charlies pushed off. I pushed off right behind them. Except for the bail bucket and the spare oar, everything on the boat was tied down twice and inaccessible. My job was to take water out of the boat as fast as I could, eight pounds at a time, and to help Jack remember which rapid was coming next and where we had decided to run it.

I saw the first of the holes in Double Drop and yelled, "Right," and we made the sneak with a dry boat. We got turned around somehow after that, though, and had to hit the big wave backwards. Jack yelled, "Hang on, baby," and we hit it straight on and it filled the boat, but then we were through it and in sight of Little Niagara before I could even start bailing.

"We're going twelve mile an hour at least, " Jack yelled. "Which one is this?"

"Niagara," I yelled. "Right center." The noise of the river swallowed my words, and I only threw out two bucketsful before we were over the lip of Niagara and I had to hold on. I could hear Ladle around the bend and I was throwing water so fast I lost my balance, and that's when I heard Jack say, "Bail faster!" and that's when I threw the bail bucket into the river and watched, unbelieving, as it went under, and I saw Jack see it too but we were at Ladle and I had to sit down and hold on. I watched Harvey's big boat getting bounced around like a cork, and I think I closed my eyes when the first wave crashed over my face because the next thing I knew we were out of the heaviest water, and Harvey was standing and smiling at us with his fist in the air.

I could see No Slouch around the bend and I don't remember it or Miranda Jane because I was kneeling in front of the boat scooping armfuls of water the whole time.

We all pulled up on the first beach we found and drank a beer and hugged each other uncertainly, like tenants in an apartment building where the fires have been put out.

"You're on your own," Harvey said. "We're camping here. Take a look at Wolf Creek, and be sure and get to shore before Selway falls." He picked up a handful of black sand and let it run through his fingers. He turned to me. "He's a good boatman, and you're very brave."

I smiled.

"Take care of each other," he said. "Stay topside."

We set off alone and it clouded up and started to rain, and I couldn't make the topography match the river map.

"I can't tell where we are," I told Jack. "But Wolf Creek can't be far."

"We'll see it coming," he said, "or hear it."

But it wasn't five minutes after he spoke that we rounded a bend and were in it, waves crashing on all sides, and Jack trying to find a way between the rocks and the holes. I was looking too, and I think I saw the run, fifty feet to our right, right before I heard Jack say, "Hang on, baby," and we hit the hole sideways and everything went white and cold. I was in the waves and underwater and I couldn't see Jack or the boat, I couldn't move my arms or legs apart from how the river tossed them. Jack had said swim down to the current, but I couldn't tell which way was down and I couldn't have moved there in that washing machine, my lungs full and taking on water. Then the wave spit me up, once, under the boat, and then again, clear of it, and I got a breath and pulled down away from the air and felt the current grab me, and I waited to get smashed against a rock, but the rock didn't come and I was at the surface riding the crests of some eight-foot rollers and seeing Jack's helmet bobbing in the water in front of me.

"Swim, baby!" he yelled, and it was like it hadn't occurred to me, like I was frozen there in the water. And I tried to swim but I couldn't get a breath and my limbs wouldn't move and I thought about the three minutes and hypothermia and I must have been swimming then because the shore started to get closer. I grabbed the corner of a big ledge and wouldn't let go, not even when Jack yelled at me to get out of the water, and even when he showed me an easy place to get out if I just floated a few yards downstream, it took all I had and more to let go of the rock and get back in the river.

I got out on a tiny triangular rock ledge, surrounded on all sides by walls of granite. Jack stood sixty feet above me on another ledge.

"Sit tight," he said. "I'm going to go see if I can get the boat."

Then he was gone and I sat in that small space and started to shake. It was raining harder, sleeting even, and I started to think about freezing to death in that space that wasn't even big enough for me to move around in and get warm. I started to think about the river rising and filling that space and what would happen when Jack got back and made me float downstream to an easier place, or what would happen if he didn't come back, if he died trying to get the boat back, if he chased it fifteen miles to Selway Falls. When I saw the boat float by, right side up and empty, I decided to climb out of the space.

I'd lost one loafer in the river, so I wedged myself between the granite walls and used my fingers, mostly, to climb. I've always been a little afraid of heights, so I didn't look down. I thought it would be stupid to live through the boating accident and smash my skull free-climbing on granite, but as I inched up the wall I got warmer and kept going. When I got to the top there were trees growing across, and another vertical bank I hadn't seen from below. I bashed through the branches with my helmet and grabbed them one at a time till they broke or pulled out and then I grabbed the next one higher. I dug into the thin layer of soil that covered the rock with my knees and my elbows, and I'd slip down an inch for every two I gained. When I came close to panic I thought of Rambo, as if he were a real person, as if what I was doing was possible, and proven before, by him.

And then I was on the ledge and I could see the river, and I could see Jack on the other side, and I must have been in shock, a little, because I couldn't at that time imagine how he could have gotten to the other side of the river, I couldn't imagine what would make him go back in the water, but he had, and there he was on the other side.

"I lost the boat," he yelled. "Walk downstream till you see it."

I was happy for instructions and I set off down the scouting trail, shoe on one foot, happy for the pain in the other, happy to be walking, happy because the sun was trying to come out again and I was there to see it. It was a few miles before I even realized that the boat would be going over the falls, that Jack would have had to swim one more time across the river to get to the trail, that I should go back and see if he'd made it, but I kept walking downstream and looking for the boat. After five miles my bare foot started to bleed, so I put my left loafer on my right foot and walked on. After eight miles I saw Jack running up the trail behind me, and he caught up and kissed me and ran on by.

I walked and I walked, and I thought about being twenty-one and hiking in mountains not too far from these with a boy who almost drowned and then proposed to me. His boots had filled with the water of a river even farther to the north, and I was wearing sneakers and have a good kick, so I made it across just fine. I thought about how he sat on the far bank after he'd pulled himself out and shivered and stared at the water. And how I ran up and down the shore looking for the shallowest crossing, and then, thinking I'd found it, met him halfway. I remember when our hands touched across the water and how I'd pulled him to safety and built him a fire and dried his clothes. Later that night he asked me to marry him, and it made me happy and I said yes even though I knew it would never happen because I was too young and free and full of my freedom. I switched my loafer to the other foot and wondered if this danger would make Jack propose to me. Maybe he was the kind of man who needed to see death first, maybe we would build a fire to dry ourselves, and then he would ask me and I would say yes because by the time you get to be thirty, freedom has circled back on itself to mean something totally different from what it did at twenty-one.

I knew I had to be close to the falls and I felt bad about what the wrecked boat would look like, but all of a sudden it was there in front of me, stuck on a gravel bar in the middle of the river with a rapid on either side, and I saw Jack coming back up the trail towards me.

"I've got it all figured out," he said. "I need to walk upstream about a mile and jump in there. That'll give me enough time to swim most of the way across to the other side of the river, and if I've read the current right, it'll take me right into that gravel bar."

"And if you read the current wrong?" I said.

He grinned. "Then it's over the Selway Falls. I almost lost it already the second time I crossed the river. It was just like Harvey said. I almost gave up. I've been running twelve miles and I know my legs'll cramp. It's a long shot but I've got to take it."

"Are you sure you want to do this?" I said. "Maybe you shouldn't do this."

"I thought the boat was gone," he said, "and I didn't care because you were safe and I was safe, and we were on the same side of the river. But there it is asking me to come for it, and the water's gonna rise tonight and take it over the falls. You stay right here where you can see what happens to me. If I make it I'll pick you up on that beach just below. We've got a half a mile to the takeout and the falls." He kissed me again and ran back upriver.

The raft was in full sunshine, everything tied down, oars in place. Even the map I couldn't read was there, where I stuck it, under a strap.

I could see Jack making his way through the trees toward the edge of the river, and I realized then that more than any other reason for being on that trip, I was there because I thought I could take care of him, and maybe there's something women want to protect after all. And maybe Jack's old girlfriends were trying to protect him by making him stay home, and maybe I thought I could if I was there, but as he dropped out of sight and into the water I knew there'd always be places he'd go that I couldn't, and that I'd have to let him go, just like the widow said. Then I saw his tiny head in the water and I held my breath and watched his position, which was perfect, as he approached the raft. But he got off center right at the end, and a wave knocked him past the raft and farther down the gravel bar. He got to his feet and went down again. He grabbed for a boulder on the bottom and got washed even farther away. He was using all his energy to stay in one place and he was fifty yards downriver from the raft. I started to pray then, to whomever I pray to when I get in real trouble, and it may have been a coincidence but he started moving forward. It took him fifteen minutes and strength I'll never know to get to the boat, but he was in it, and rowing, and heading for the beach.

Later, when we were safe and on the two-lane heading home, Jack told me we were never in any real danger, and I let him get away with it because I knew that's what he had to tell himself to get past almost losing me.

"The river gave us both a lesson in respect," he said, and it occurred to me then that he thought he had a chance to tame that wild river, but I knew I was at its mercy from the very beginning, and I thought all along that that was the point.

Jack started telling stories to keep himself awake: the day his kayak held him under for almost four minutes, the time he crashed his hang glider twice in one day. He said he thought fifteen years of highwater was probably enough, and that he'd take desert rivers from now on.

The road stretched out in front of us, dry and even and smooth. We found a long dirt road, turned, and pulled down to where it ended at a chimney that stood tall amid the rubble of an old stone house. We didn't build a fire and Jack didn't propose; we rolled out our sleeping bags and lay down next to the truck. I could see the light behind the mountains in the place where the moon would soon rise, and I thought about all the years I'd spent saying love and freedom were mutually exclusive and living my life as though they were exactly the same thing.

The wind carried the smell of the mountains, high and sweet. It was so still I could imagine a peace without boredom.

Animals as Brothers and Sisters

Brenda Peterson

As a child I played a game with my siblings: *What country are you? What body of water? What war? What animal?* My sister was Ireland, the South Seas, the War of Independence, and a white stallion. My brother was Timbuktu, the Amazon River, the One Hundred Years War, and a cobra. I was South America, the Gulf of Mexico, the Civil War, and a dolphin. Sometimes we called upon our animals — my sister galloping away from grown-ups with a powerful snort and a flick of her fine, silver mane; my brother summoning the fierce serpent hiss to ward off his older sisters; and I, soaring through sea and air with my tribe of dolphins.

Our parents didn't think it odd then that their children metamorphosed into animals, oceans, or wars right there in the middle of the living room or backyard. My father always planted his family next to a forest, a river, or an ocean — all of which were expansive and natural enough to absorb our wildest play. One of the few times our transformation was curbed was at the dinner table — if, say, my brother as cobra poised above my hand as I cut the cake in exact equal pieces or if my sister was pawing the tablecloth with her pale equine impatience.

Then my father, whose own play was raising horses and hunting, might threaten my sister with a tight bit or suggest my brother uncoil himself and cool down until his blood was really reptilian, slow and grounded.

"The cobra can't uncoil until he strikes and eats," my brother would mutter as he sighed and right before us changed back into the youngest child. But his eyes remained hooded.

"The white stallion is never broken," my sister would warn my father, who did raise her with a freer hand as if she were one of his fine, high-strung thoroughbreds.

I was always under water during these discussions, in the green, shady depths of my warm gulf, listening more intently to a language that creaked and chattered like high speed hinges — dolphin gossip. Or sometimes I just tuned in to their other language: the pictures dolphins send one another in their minds. Because I had to come up for air, and my eyes were as good above water as below, I did keep a lookout on my family's dinner dramas. But if my mother was having one of her bad moods or my father was giving his lectures, back down I'd go to my other family, who welcomed me with wide-open fins. Even without hands, the dolphins embraced me more than most people did. It was body-to-body, full embrace, our eyes unblinking, utterly open as we swam, belly-to-belly, our skin twenty times more sensitive than that of humans.

The play my siblings and I chose as children is mirrored in the way we live as grown-ups. And I suspect it has much to do with our career choices, our relationships, even where we choose to live. My sister finds her South Seas body of water (and reunites with our family's Seminole blood) by living in Florida and marrying into an old Key West family. She is still fighting her War of Independence, a ripsnorting battle, which involves her husband and three daughters as high-spirited playmates. Every so often I see her snort and toss her full mane of hair; and when she really means business, she paws the ground with her delicate, high-heeled hooves. My brother, as a Navy jet navigator, has traveled the world, is caught up in all sorts of military intrigue in far places — enough to last one hundred years easy. His serpentine ways have surrendered more to the feminine aspects of the snake, for at the births of his two daughters, my brother shed his toughened military skin and was reborn. And me, well I now live in a whole city under water: Seattle. And I'm still swimming with dolphins.

This is difficult to do in Puget Sound with its year-round temperature variation from forty-six to forty-eight degrees Fahrenheit. So aside from sighting dolphin schools from shore or ferry, I've had to go to warmer waters to make my psychic life match up with my actual life. How convenient then that my sister's Conch Republic connections carried me to the Florida Keys to find my animal allies.

Actually, it was a kind of coincidence. Four years ago I was sitting in my Seattle study listening to the splatter of rain on my roof, reading a *New York Times* article about a Florida Keys research program that reversed our society's usual prejudice against animals: the dolphins were not there for human amusement. Instead, we were their "toys," and the researchers studied the interaction between humans and dolphins while in the cetacean's own environment. Everything was geared toward what fascinated the dolphins, what made them choose a particular person as a swimming partner over another. Researchers don't know why, but dolphins prefer children first, then women, and then men. But why do they ignore some people completely and gather around others with absolute attention?

As I was reading this article, my sister Paula called. Seems she was stranded in a motel along the string of coral keys, en route to Key West. I could just hear her champing at the bit. "We're stuck here overnight. The girls are bored silly," she said. They weren't the only ones, I suggested, then told her about the dolphin research that just happened to be only miles from their motel.

"All right, all right, we'll go swim with your dolphins," Paula said.

My sister was eight months pregnant with her third daughter, and none of her deliveries had been simple. That's why my sister, lowering herself and her swollen belly into the warm tropical water, showed her true mettle — she was, as my father always recognized, fine, greathearted horseflesh. My nieces needed no courage to dive into the lagoons where dolphins chattered about them. It was delight at first sight.

These dolphins are in "elective captivity," which means the underwater fences that separate them from the saltwater canal leading to the ocean are opened twice a day to let the dolphins return to their home territory. They return to the research center of their own free will. No dolphin has ever chosen to escape: they seem as fascinated with humans as we are with them, though we've given them much reason to keep their distance. There is no record, since antiquity, of a dolphin harming humans; yet we routinely kill thousands of dolphin every year with our tuna industry's tactics of drift-net fishing. In our search for tuna, our nets trap hundreds of dolphins a day. They die dreadfully; they drown.

Because dolphins breathe as we do, nurse their young, and are warm-blooded, there is a mammalian bond, which perhaps explains why dolphins have anything whatsoever to do with humans. The bond was evident as Paula lost her pregnant waddle and floated weightless, waiting for the dolphins. But first they played with her daughters. My four-year-old niece, Lauren, with the fierce grip of all newborns and single-minded children, grabbed hold of a dorsal fin and held on as she was sped around the lagoon at what seemed like the speed of light. She doesn't remember seeing anything but bright bubbles. Careful to keep Lauren's small head above water, her dolphin, who weighed about three hundred pounds and was itself a relative child (only six years old in a life span of approximately forty years), carried Lauren as it would a precious baby doll.

Another dolphin swam sister Lindsay, two and a half, round and round until she was dizzy. Then they let her bob about in her life jacket, singing at the top of her lungs. The dolphins showed their approval with some tail slaps, spins, and leaps, always careful about their motors, those great tails. With their phenomenal 360-degree overlapping vision, the dolphins always know exactly where you are. After playing with the children, the dolphins circled my sister, and when their echolocation heard the fetal heartbeat, they got very excited. The high-frequency whines and creaks increased as their sonar sounded my sister's belly, read the fetal blood pressure, and scanned the infant's stomach gases for signs of stress.

"What are they doing?" Paula asked. Her whole body was buzzing.

"Offering to midwife you," the researcher replied. "They seem concerned about the baby. Is…is there anything wrong?"

"I don't think so," Paula answered, and for the first time in that lagoon, she felt fear. My sister is a nurse and knows all about ultrasound. But perhaps there was something the dolphins deciphered that our technology didn't.

Then the researcher told my nieces how the dolphins midwife one another, assisting the mother as she swirls and spins in labor by stroking her flanks and at the moment of birth, when the newborn dolphin eases out of one watery womb into another, the midwives lift the calf with their long, sensitive beaks up to the surface. There the newborn dolphin takes its first breath. Every breath thereafter for the rest of the dolphin's life will be taken consciously. A cetacean's brain, somewhat larger than that of a human's, has had thirty million more years of evolutionary development than our species. Some scientists theorize the dolphins exist in an alpha state — what we experience as meditation — and since they never really sleep, just switch sides of the brain being used, researchers wonder what kind of intelligence is here.

My sister certainly wondered when she gave birth three weeks later to a daughter with a rare blood disease. Had the dolphins diagnosed it? After much trauma and weeks of watching her newborn double as a tiny human pincushion, Paula brought her daughter, Lissie, home from the hospital.

On Lissie's second birthday, in gratitude and out of curiosity, we took her back to swim with dolphins. But the rules had changed: no pregnant women and only children who are excellent swimmers. So little Lissie jumped and leaped on the side of the lagoon, shouting, "I am a dolphin! I am a dolphin!" as her sisters and Paula and I all slipped back into the warm salt water. This was my second swim with dolphins, and my first time at the Dolphins Plus Marine Mammal Research & Education Center in Key Largo. My dolphin companions, Niki, Dreamer, and Sara, were six-year-old females in elective captivity only two years. Exuberant, still quite wild, they were children themselves.

"Remember," our researcher reminded us as we eased into the water, "you'll have to be creative if you want them to play with you — don't just bob about gawking. They've already got enough float toys."

The dolphins here are not rewarded with food for interaction with humans; that is the old model of performance. Food is given the dolphins at another time, separate from human-cetacean interaction. The real reward for all of us is the play itself.

As I swam, snorkel mask down, arms at my side to signal that I would wait for them to choose to play with me, I heard far below the familiar high-frequency dialogue. It sounded like the high-pitched whine of a jet engine right before takeoff, combined with rapid creaks and bleeps. The sounds encircled my body and then, as the dolphins came closer, there was that astonishing physical sensation of being probed by their sonar. It's as subtle as an X ray, but exhilarating. My whole body tingled, stomach gurgled, head felt pleasurable pricking as if a high-speed ping-pong game played with light was bouncing around my brain.

I am reminded of my friend John Carlyle, who has researched, trained, and played with dolphins for twenty years, telling me of one of his experiments with dolphin echolocation. Trying to discern the limits of dolphin sonar, he placed eyecups on his dolphins and then asked them to recognize certain symbols by echolocation. In an experiment that had taken him months to design, the dolphins learned the symbols in five minutes. So John had to come up with more difficult ways of testing the depth of their sonar. After much research, his final experiment, which was the limit of human technology at the time, discovered dolphins could discern a symbol one one-thousandth of an inch square; they could also differentiate varying carbon densities in metal rods, and distinguish colors — all by echolocation. Knowing of their precision made the experience of having my body echo-scrutinized more than simply a physical sensation. I was scanned more profoundly than by anything our medical science has yet invented. But there is another element here, not at all scientific. It is what happens to my heart, not physiologically, but emotionally.

Every time I'm sounded by a cetacean, I feel as if my cells are penetrated, seen, and — what is most remarkable — accepted. I've never felt judgment, even if the dolphin chose to bypass me for another playmate. The Dolphins Plus researchers report that often, whether a dolphin spends five or forty-five minutes with a swimmer, that person will say it was enough, all they needed, as much as they could receive. In fact, every time I've swum with dolphins, my human companions have admitted afterward that we each felt like the favorite. Could it be we have something to learn about parenting from dolphins?

As I swam on the surface, peering through my mask into the dense green depth, I wondered what I must look like to a dolphin. Humans are the most ungainly mammals dolphins see in the ocean. We are the only creatures in the sea who splash at both ends of our bodies. Our appendages don't move in sync with the sea as do the long arms of anemones. There is only one dance in the sea, one pulsing movement of all that lives, one law. Even if one of our bombs exploded here, its harm would be muted. And after it exploded, its metal innards would settle to the sea bottom as no more than an artificial reef adorned by pink brain coral, starfish, and barnacles. Swimming and hoping a dolphin might play with me, I wondered about those ancient dolphin ancestors who decided millions of years ago — while humans were still hanging from trees — to go back to the sea. Did those early cetaceans foresee the fate of our species' self-destruction? Is that why they left us to our weapon-and-tool-making hands (the use of which takes up so much of our brain's functions), while their skeletal hands slowly evolved into flippers to flow *with* rather then change their environment?

The dolphins always come when I'm most distracted, when my mind is not on them at all, but drifting, perhaps dreaming. In my floating reverie, I was startled by the sensuous skin stroking my legs. I happily recognized the silken, clean, elegant feel of dolphin belly as Dreamer ran her whole body across my back like a bow glides across violin strings. And then she was gone. There were only the sounds fading, then coming closer as suddenly all three young dolphins swam toward me. I still see in my dreams those gray globelike domes with brown, unblinking eyes meeting mine as the dolphins greeted me under water. "Intimate" is the only way I can describe their eye contact. Benevolent, familiar, and again that acceptance. Any fear one feels vanishes once those eyes hold yours.

"Choose one!" the researcher shouted above me. Having been under water so long, I could barely hear his voice. But I remembered his instructions; the dolphins are possessive of their toys and I must bond with only one or else they'd squabble among themselves. So I chose Niki, though Dreamer was my favorite, because if truth be told, Niki made the choice. She slipped her dorsal fin under my arm and raced off with me at such a speed I saw only bubbles and sky. Then she dove with me and we both held our breaths. As we surfaced, I saw in the opposite lagoon two dolphins leaping with my nieces like calves in tow. No time to see anything else — I inhaled and dove down again.

Thrilling, this underwater ballet, as I twirled with my dolphin, my hands along her flanks. Fluid, this liquid life below where all is weightless and waves of warmth enfolded my body as I breathed air in this watery element. And I was not alone. Everywhere was sound — my nieces singing, and the dolphins' dialogue. My mind suddenly filled with pictures. Then I realized that every time I imagined my dolphin doing something, a split second later she did it. It was not a performance at my request; it was an answer to my wondering. Call and response. It was also an anticipation of my delight, a willingness that is the purest form of play.

I pictured myself spinning round, one hand on Niki's heart — it happened. I saw both my arms outstretched, a dolphin's dorsal offered each hand — and suddenly I was flying between Niki and Dreamer. It was impossible to tell who was sending whom these pictures. But they all happened. It was like instant replay of everything imagined. And now I understood why the child in me chose dolphins. What more perfect playmates?

Ahead in the water swam my sister. Paula was galloping with her dolphin; and my niece Lauren had a dolphin gently resting its long beak on her legs like a paddle to push her through the water. Distracted, I broke one of the basic rules: I got too close to a dolphin and her favorite toy (Paula). Suddenly a wallop to my shoulder. My world turned upside down and though I was face-up in the air, I breathed water. Sputtering, I broke another rule: my body tilted vertically, a sign to the dolphins of distress. Another whack of a pectoral in the lower back, then a beak thrust under my bottom to raise me above the water.

"Horizontal!" the researchers yelled. "They think you're drowning."

I would rather play with a dolphin than be rescued by one. Those whacks are painful reprimands, a lesson in life and death to a wayward human. Blowholes fiercely expelled their air everywhere around me. Surrounded by all three dolphins, I started to cry. I failed, I felt. I was a fool. And for the first time ever, I was afraid of them.

It was hard not to cower there in the water with them. All the pictures flooding my mind overwhelmed me and I couldn't figure anything out. Except I remembered to float, though my body was rigid and what I would most have liked to do was curl up into a fetal ball and be safe on shore the way long ago I'd surface from my own darker daydreams to find myself at the comfortingly ordinary dinner table I first sought to escape. But this was real; I couldn't imagine my way out of it. Or could I?

Again and again one picture in my head. It was I, still shaken, but surrendering to all three dolphins at once. I breathed raggedly, the snorkel like an intruding fist into my mouth. But after closing my eyes, I allowed it. Yes, they could come back and find me again where I floated in fear. At first Niki and Sara were tentative, their beaks very gently stroking my legs. Now that I wasn't going to drown, would I play with them again?

I am small, I thought, and hoped they could hear. *I am just a human being — afraid and fragile in your element. Be careful with me?*

And they were. Together the three of them floated me so slowly my body barely rippled water. Then began the deepest healing. Dreamer gently eased me away from the others with a nudge of her dorsal fin. Her eyes steadily held mine as she swam gracefully in wide arcs of figure eights around the lagoon. In and out through warm water. My body surrendered to the massage, not of hands, but of water and sound. I thought of the others who come here who are not as healthy as I — the autistic and Down's syndrome children, the handicapped, the terminally ill, all of whom are nursed by the dolphins who embraced me. Deeper than the play, more moving than the sense of another mind in these waters, was the simple kindness of the creatures. I did not understand it. I wanted to.

When I closed my eyes, the pictures grew stronger, as did my senses. My hands slid down Dreamer's silken body, memorizing notches and scars as a blind woman does her loved one. I remembered that in China those born blind were believed to be the most gifted masseurs — because hands are another way of seeing. My hands still hold the exact feel of dolphin skin. Even now, across time and continent, my hands can still grow warmer, tingle with the memory of that cool, sleek skin that trembles when touched.

Dreamer's name comes from her eyes. Half-lidded, there is in her mild, dark eyes a different light. Sloe-eyed, they call it down South —

and the sweet, fizzy drink made from those black sloe berries is a euphoric mix reminiscent of humid, fragrant Southern nights. *Down home*, I thought, as we glided through dark green depths. I closed my eyes and felt that this underwater world, too, was down home.

As Dreamer circled with me, I was so relaxed I barely recognized the voices far above in the high, harsher air. "Come back," the researcher called. "It's time…but the dolphins are having so much fun with you, they're not going to let you get out easily."

There was a firmness to our researcher's voice, like a parent calling children in from play. We'd been swimming with the dolphins three times longer than the allotted half hour and I suddenly realized I was utterly exhausted. I felt like I'd been moving heavy furniture for days. My snorkel mask fogged and the balmy wind felt abrupt. I remembered gravity and how it works against me.

"You'll all have to link arms to signal the dolphins that you're serious about getting out. They'll respect your tribe. But they'll protest!"

As my sister and my nieces and I moved toward the dock, the dolphins leapt over our heads, chided us for spoiling their sport, and swam figure eights between our legs. Even as we hoisted ourselves up onto the platform, Niki cajoled my niece by opening her long beak and running it up and down Lauren's small leg.

"She's testing you," the researcher told Lauren and laughed. "They only do that when they *really* like you."

"It's a compliment," Lauren confirmed in her most matter-of-fact voice. "She likes me best."

Of course we all secretly felt that way. I still feel that way, these many months later as I sit surrounded by my photos — Dreamer's eyes still hold mine as she glides by in a shining green background; Niki exuberantly leaps above the surface; Sara offers her abiding companionship. My niece Lauren sends me drawings of dolphins and whales; her sister Lindsay has decided to speak nothing but dolphin dialect when I call long-distance. We cluck and click and make sounds deep in our throats like a Geiger counter. Anyone crossing wires on our conversations might think there was electronic equipment trouble on the line.

So the second generation of our family carries on the tradition of claiming our animals within. I often tell my nieces a story about the

Northwest Coast Indian belief that before humans came on the scene, the world was made up of beings whose spirits could change into anything from salmon to rock, from raven to waterfall. Every form had its lessons. And the human form, being the most recent, was considered to have the most lessons. Long ago, when my own father taught me that animals were part of our larger family, he echoed this common wisdom. It is wisdom that still serves me well.

For example, I'll often find myself in some situation thinking: "What would a dolphin do?" Animals do not change the world; they adapt. In my own life, the flexibility and adaptability of a dolphin mind, the sense of tribe and play, guides me. I can call upon the dolphin inside me for counsel as well as companionship. And the irony is that apprenticing myself to an animal like a cetacean somehow teaches me more about becoming a human being. As John Lilly, the respected dolphin researcher, wrote, "You see, what I found after twelve years of work with dolphins, is that the limits are not in them, the limits are in us. So I had to go away and find out, who am I? What's this all about?"

These days here in the Northwest, where the Puget Sound offers some of the world's most fertile habitat for marine animals, I realize that becoming a dolphin, like becoming a human, is a state of mind. Here, where the Native Americans remind us that everything shimmers with its own inner life, I walk by the water and send greetings in the form of mental pictures to all the mammals that swim in the Sound. Often I visit the belugas at Point Defiance Zoo, especially when I am sad or in need of inspiration. Those white, generous creatures gaze at me through glass and I put my hands up, hoping they'll feel my own little form of echolocation. Sometimes I sing to them and they give back with resonant mews and trills.

On a recent visit I was lucky enough to make physical contact with Maya and Inouk, the zoo's two older belugas. Each took my hand deep into its great mouth, by way of tasting and greeting me. Their soft pink tongues clasped my hand as their melons (those dazzling white globelike foreheads) subtly changed size and shape to scan me. It felt like they held the whole of me, their eyes on mine, as they gently took my hand. For days afterward, my hands tingled with warmth.

If I am to learn to live by water, what better teacher than a cetacean? If my brother and sisters are across a continent from me, what better siblings than marine mammal kin? And if I am to metamorphose and try to transform my life into what as a child I only dreamed about, what better myths to live by than the Northwest Indian stories that tell of mysterious beings who metamorphose back and forth between animal and human kingdoms?

In my study, next to my wall of Dreamer, Niki, and Sara photos, between my whale mobile and drawing of a purple Grandmother Whale drawn by my niece Lauren, is a small black-and-white sketch of a woman swimming upstream, her body half salmon. Entwined in a surging school of salmon, she leaps and insists herself toward her homeland. Drawn by Caroline Orr, a local Colville tribal member and native painter, this inspired storytelling-in-art reminds me of all the other worlds that coexist alongside me: Salmon People's world, the sky world, this Sound's watery world. Maybe I can learn to swim between them. After all, Native Americans know that salmon are really people who live in underwater villages. It is these people who graciously change into fish each spring to give us our food.

Sometimes staring long enough at Orr's *Raven and Salmon Woman*, I feel silver scales glisten against my sides and am emboldened by the bravery of a being who seeks her birthplace while making the circle of death and renewal. Sometimes gazing into Dreamer's familiar eyes as she swims toward me, my room full of windows becomes an air-filled aquarium. And sometimes when Seattle is so low and gray, the misting rain so familiar, I know we human mammals here in the Northwest underwater villages are closely related to the Salmon People, the cetaceans, and all life in the sea.

Each of us has an animal totem, some are blessed with many. We can all summon our animals and they will come. They will be our brothers and sisters and live alongside us — even swim upstream to die with us so we will not be without a guide through that greatest change of worlds. Some myths say that our animals then enter other afterlife dimensions with us, and return to begin this Earth's journey all over again.

I know that claiming cetaceans as my kin is not just science, it's shrewd. Learning to be human and to know what I might become, I need all the help I can get.

The local storyteller Johnny Moses (Nuu Chah Nulth tribe) told this Salish tale at a gathering:

> Long ago the trees thought they were people.
> Long ago the mountains thought they were people.
> Long ago the animals thought they were people.
> Someday they will say…
> Long ago the human beings thought they were people.

"Waiting For the Parade #3," Etching by George Johanson, 1985.

Northwest Passage

David James Duncan

When I was sixteen and hated high school, one of the things I used to do to get through a school day was rip pictures out of magazines. I'd do this in the school library, and the magazines belonged to the school: the ripping was a deliberate act of vandalism. But I only stole photos I loved. And at the time I felt that, in taking them home to my bedroom, I was stealing them away to a better life than the one they'd led in the library.

I had decorated my bedroom with hanging blankets, cheap imported tapestries, wooden crates, lanterns, and sheepskins, so that it looked more like the interior of a desert Bedouin's tent than the generic, Sheet-rocked cubicle it was. And when I got my stolen photos into my "tent" I'd place them on the wall above my desk, light candles or kerosene wicks beneath them, stare at them till they swallowed me, and virtually worship the daydreams and longings this process allowed me to feel.

One such photo, plundered from a *National Geographic,* was of the confluence of the Ganges and Jumna rivers in India. It depicted a barren, boulder-strewn plateau beneath mountainous terrain. You could see white water churning in the background. But the place was stripped of vegetation, desolate, and would have held no photographic interest at all if the rocky plain along the river hadn't been strewn with huts. *Hundreds* of huts. Maybe a thousand of them. Crude, leaky, diminutive hovels no red-blooded American would dream of keeping even a lawnmower in. Yet in these, men were living. "Holy men," the caption called them. In any case long-bearded, huge-eyed, emaciated men, just existing on the rocks by the river there. And the reason they chose to do this, so the caption maintained, was that "the rishis of ancient India considered the confluence of two or more rivers to be a sacred place."

I couldn't explain, even to myself, why I found this riverside ghetto so appealing. Trying to hone in on my feelings with the help of a dictionary, I looked up the word holy and in the margins of the photo wrote, "1. hallowed by association with the divine, hence deserving of reverence, 2. inviolable; not to be profaned." But weeks passed and understanding did not deepen. I was still in a kind of love with the confluence-dwelling holy men, and still unable to say why, when an old friend named Jered asked me to go fishing.

It was the morning of a school day in mid-October when Jered asked me. His plan was to try for jack and silver salmon that very afternoon — which we would lengthen slightly by cutting our last class. Jered and I had been fishing buddies as kids, inseparable for a season or two. In the years between I prided myself on having changed completely, while Jered prided himself on not having changed at all. I'd become a hippie; Jered still had a crewcut; I aspired (with no success) to vegetarianism; Jered was still shooting, cleaning, and happily devouring scores of the indigenous mammals and birds of the Northwest; I was anti-war; Jered was pro-obedience; I was trying to piece together some sort of crazy-quilt Bhakti/Wishram/Buddhistic/ballplaying mysticism to live by; Jered was your basic working-class, Consciousness One, Huntin' n' Fishin' type guy. But I said yes for three reasons. The first was that we shared a mutual respect, despite our growing differences, based on the fact that we each considered the other to be the best fisherman we knew. The second was that he had enough boraxed salmon roe for both of us, and the fishing had been, in his rudimentary but reliable diction, "hot." And the third reason, the decisive one, was that the place he proposed to take us was one the rishis of ancient India held sacred: a joining of rivers — this one in downtown Camas, Washington, where Lackamas Creek and the Washougal met the Columbia, and the Crown Zellerbach papermill met them all.

I knew, before going, that this confluence would be a place I would hate. I'd lived within sight and smell of the Crown Z mill, directly across the Columbia, all my life. My plan for the day though — having read of the ancient rishis — was to see whether it might be possible to love what I would hate as well.

To get to our confluence we drove half an hour down the Oregon side of the Columbia, half an hour back up the Washington side, parked in the Crown Z visitors' lot, ignored the No Trespassing and High Voltage and Danger signs, passed through a hole in a cyclone fence, detoured round a gigantic mill building, crossed disused railroad tracks and bull-dozed fields, reached the Washougal's last long riffle, clambered downstream through brambles and scrub willow, eased in alongside another huge mill wall, and came to a kind of bay. The confluence proper — the exact spot where the crystal-clear Washougal blended with the complicated greens of the Columbia — turned out to be a slow, fishy-looking glide directly below the mill wall and just at the neck of the bay.

The river bank there was interesting: it was made of hardpacked clay, bare rock, spilled oil, logging cable, shards of every kind and color of pop, beer, and booze bottle, flood-crushed car and appliance parts, slabs of broken concrete with rebar sticking out of them, driftwood, drift Styrofoam, drift tires, and reject mill-parts — *huge* reject mill-parts.

We found a rusted sprocket the size of a merry-go-round and sat on it.

Our legs fit perfectly between the teeth.

We had come, I felt in my very center, to a confluence of everything that created, sustained and warped us. The question was: was it a viable home? Was it still somehow holy? Or was I, with my Bedouin bedroom and stolen Oriental photos, right to long only for escape?

We began setting up the odd tackle we'd both come to prefer as boys: a stiff fiberglass flyrod and light spinning reel (mine open-faced, his closed); monofilament line, for length of cast, a third the test of that used by most salmon fishermen. There wasn't a holy man in sight. There wasn't any kind of human in sight. The mill rumbled behind us like an insatiable stomach; tugs dragged log rafts up Crown Z's own private slough; a dredge worked the slough a half-mile down river; trucks and cars whished along the jettied highway across the bay; ships and barges plowed the Columbia beyond. It was the machines you saw and heard though, not the people inside them. Industrial men, not holy ones. Them's the kind we grow in these parts.

Yet it was still beautiful at the confluence. We could see east to the Cascade foothills, west clear to the Coast Range, and an enormous piece of Oregon lay across the river to the south. And there is a Gangian majesty to the lower Columbia, and something awesome, if not holy, in knowing its currents are made of the glaciers, springs, desert seeps, and dark industrial secrets of two Canadian provinces and six American states. When I kept my eyes on distant vistas, or on the two waters blending at our feet, I could even imagine the possibility of some kind of "association with the divine" here. Though I'd no faith in the wisdom of the resident machine operators, I could imagine Indians, the American kind, watching these same mountains while awaiting these same fish, some of them maybe knowing what the rishis once knew.

But when I finally tried, as I had known I must, to incorporate the third waterway into the picture, things broke down: Lackamas Creek — a genuine little river — entered the uphill side of the Crown Zellerbach mill; it headed in the mountains north of Camas, and had its own run of salmon, once. But the mill-used fluid that shot from the flume at our feet bore no resemblance to water. It looked like hot pancake batter, gushing forth in a quantity so vast and foul that part of me found it laughable. It looked like Satan's own nostril risen from hell, blowing out an infinite, scalding booger. But it was a steaming, poisonous, killing joke that shot across the Washougal's drought-shriveled mouth in a yellow-gray scythe, curved downstream, and coated the Columbia's north shore with what looked like dead human skin for miles. And maybe a rishi could have pondered this and still felt some equanimity. All I could feel, though, just as I'd feared, was fury and impotence and sickness. I said nothing to Jered — who had merely grabbed his nose once, said "*Pyoo!*" and set about fishing. I just squeezed my eyes shut, tried the same with my brain, and waited for my friend to give up and take us elsewhere. But I couldn't help but hear the flume's diarrheal gushing.

And then, over the gushing, a strange double splash.

The first half of the splash was a bright coho salmon. The second half was its echo, bouncing so hard off the mill wall behind us that I turned to the sound, half expecting to see yet another river running through the rubble and broken glass.

"*Look!*" Jered whispered as a second bright coho leapt high in the evening light, fell back in the river — and again the loud, clean echo. Then another one leapt, and another, all amazingly high, all in the same place — a point in midriver, just upstream from the scythe.

My first impulse, lip-service vegetarianism and all, was to grab my rod. A big school of silvers was clearly moving in. But Jered, the unashamed carnivore, had stopped fishing. He was just watching and listening now. And though I would not have done the same if he hadn't set the example, I too grew satisfied to watch — for those salmon leaps were language: they were the salmon people's own legend, enacted before our eyes. And though we'd heard the old story a thousand times, though we knew it by rote, it was being given a twist, at this confluence, that we two sons of these same troubled waters needed to sit still and hear.

The familiar part of the story, the rote chorus, told how these unlikely creatures had been born way up this mountain river, had grown strong in it, then had left it for the Pacific; yet some impression of their birthplace, some memory of scent touched them years and leagues later in that vastness, brought them schooling in off the Columbia's mouth, forced them to run the gauntlet of nets, hooks, and predators, search the big river's murky greens, solve the riddle, and enter again the waters of their fatal, yet life-giving, home. Then came the twist — in the shape of a scythe.

Salmon are not stupid. They grow tentative in rivers. They know when to spook, and when to wait quietly; when to leap, when to hide, when to fight for their lives. As these coho entered their confluence and tasted the scythe they must surely have tried everything — must have hesitated, sought another channel, circled back out into the Columbia, come round again and again, waiting for the pain of the thing to diminish; for rain to fall; rivers to rise; industries to die. But like all indigenous species, including in the end our own, salmon have no choice: their great speed and long journeys create an illusion of freedom, but to live as a race they must finally become as much a part of their river as its water and its stones. So in the end, they entered. With eyes that can't close and breath that can't be held they darted straight into this confounding of the vast, the pure, and the insane. And the slashing leaps that now shattered the river's surface were each the coho word for their cold, primordial rage against whatever it was that maimed them — and their equally cold, primordial joy at having reached the waters of their home.

So we never did fish that day, Jered and I. We just sat like a couple of Ganges River hut-jockeys on a reject mill-sprocket, watching salmon leap as the day grew dark. Yet after each leap my breath would catch as the splash resounded, impossibly loud, against the walls of the mill and the surface-rings tripled, at least for an instant, the two dimensions of the killing scythe. Feeling a frail hope welling inside me, feeling a need to memorize, for life, this same wild leap and passage, I suddenly began to dread my old fishing partner — or to dread, at least, the Consciousness One, Huntin' n' Fishin' type summary I expected him to make at any moment, thus crewcutting the beauty off of all that we were seeing.

But when I finally did turn to my stick-in-the-mud friend, he didn't even notice me. And in his eyes, which were brimming, I saw nothing but that same cold anger, and that same wild joy. Jered was not watching fish jump. He was raging and exulting with the coho as if they were our people; as if ours were the ancient instincts that had sorted the Columbia's countless strands, ours the unclosing eyes the scythe betrayed and blinded, ours the bright bodies leaping and falling back into the home waters — falling just to burst them apart; just to force them to receive, even now, our gleaming silver sides.

Holy Water

Jessica Maxwell

We'd been fishing about five minutes when a cannibal wind came screaming out of the north and started slapping our rowboat around. Then the early morning aspic of Discovery Passage blew up in our faces, splattering the air with violent black stew. It happened in seconds. It always does up there on the 50th parallel in that narrow raceway between Vancouver and Quadra Islands off the fractured coast of British Columbia, a place joined at the latitudinal hip with England's Land's End, Newfoundland, and Siberia. January, August — it doesn't matter. The local Kwagiulth Indians knew that at any moment the Cannibal at the North End of the World could hiss his icy breath south and turn their sacred fishing grounds into a real man-eater.

Rich sucked the rain out of his mustache. "Thirteen pulls," he said, but the wind ate his words. I had fished this demented water a hundred times, so I took a guess and sunk a dozen arm lengths of line into that evil bucking soup, praying that Rich's double-clinch knot and his antique Lucky Louie lure would have a lasting relationship. I also prayed that I would, after all these years, finally fish myself into The Tyee Club of British Columbia.

The Tyee Club was founded in 1924 by exceptionally sporting anglers who realized that exceptional fish need exceptional protection from run-of-the-mill yayhoos who would take every last one by any means possible if you let them. So the Club laid down a few ground rules to give the colossal salmon I have personally pursued for the better part of a decade "a sporting chance." Under Tyee Club regulations you can, for instance, only fish out of a rowboat — no motors allowed. You may use only a hand operated reel, your line must have a breaking strength of twenty pounds or less, and you are allowed only a single hook, artificial trolling lure-bait is strictly forbidden. And the only way to get into the Tyee Club is to boat a thirty-pounder or better "tyee" salmon using regulation tackle and tactics. After nine years and God knows how many tides, I had only managed to land an infuriating twenty-eight and a half-pounder. Thus had I become a woman possessed, and no stinking Cannibal breath was going to keep me off the holy water that Indian and non-Indian alike call the Tyee Pool.

Tyee is a word borrowed from the old Chinook jargon used between Indians and early white traders all along the Northwest coast. It means "chief," and that's what the original tribes named the biggest Pacific salmon, the species we now call "king" or "chinook." It was no overstatement. For at least 8,500 years — 4,000 years before the pyramids were built — Pacific Northwest Indians counted on salmon like we count on McDonald's. So when a Kwagiulth fisherman handlined a sixty-pound tyee into his dugout canoe, you can bet he was humming his version of "Hail to the Chief."

Some of British Columbia's biggest tyee have come out of the Tyee Pool, the wide, shallow mouth of the Campbell River. The river empties into Discovery Passage just beneath the nipple of Vancouver Island's long, lean east coast, some 170 road miles north of Victoria. If you ever happen to snorkel down the Campbell, you'll see why it produces such lunkers. Thanks to the filtering action of upstream waterfalls, the river bed is filled with fist sized rocks. Cobble rock, they call it. And since spawning female salmon dig their nests, or redds, some seventeen inches into the gravel, the old Campbell self-selected eons ago for big mothers with Terminator-tails. The result was a run of tyee that routinely weighed-in at forty, fifty, even seventy pounds per — tens of pounds larger than the salmon of neighboring rivers.

Fossils prove that salmonoids have run in the Northwest for five million years, the wily survivors of many Ice Ages. Ever since the last one about 11,000 years ago, Campbell River salmon have spent their summer vacations cruising the Tyee Pool while they transmogrified from salt water predators into fresh water spawning machines; which is why

Rich Chapple, tyee fishing guide extraordinaire, and I were sitting in a boat the size of a damn hot tub half an hour before sunrise, fishing blind in weather that could rip the fur off of King Kong — all for the love of these impertinent fish that have about as much interest in eating as Dick Gregory.

"Whoa!" Rich hollered as one porpoised and rolled inches from our boat. Its splash spritzed me in the face. It tasted like oysters. "That's good luck," Rich yelled and he ought to know. In his early guiding career, he used to eat the heart of every tyee his clients caught — raw. Tyee salmon are, in fact, almost impossible to catch. That's because they are interested in sex, not food. By the time they enter the dilute saline liquor of the Tyee Pool, their stomachs have shrunk to the size of a lug nut as their bodies filled with the procreational cargo needed for the lusty last act of their lives. It is an aggressive, if sub-gustatory, time in a salmon's life. Males fight males for mates, females prepare to defend their once and future redds. Thus, an angler's only chance is to bonk an already semi-pissed-off tyee on the head with a ridiculous imitation of a squid or a herring and hope the little Pliocene devil bites it out of sheer irritability.

In Discovery Passage, the morning tide is usually an ebb like the one Rich was fighting. Ebb tides there move north faster than you can row, so there we were, sitting in Lucky, Rich's rowboat, doing what's called an "ebb drift," where you start at the south end of The Tyee Pool and row hard against the current but still drift northward along the edge of The Bar, an underwater sandy ridge where the big boys like to stop by for a cold one.

It takes a lot of skill to row an ebb, especially in cannibal weather. That's why it's so important to have a guide who knows what he or she is doing. You also want a guide with a good collection of classic tyee tackle who knows which plug or spoon to row on which tide and how to row it.

Tyee tackle is one of the sport's great mysteries. A tyee angler cannot, for instance, gather together fifty kinds of hackle and herl and whip up a Jock Scott fly guaranteed to attract the bejeeses out of an Atlantic salmon and expect it to have the same effect on a British Columbia tyee. It won't. Nothing will. Attraction has nothing to do with it. Aggravation does, which is why the Quasimodo spaz-attacks of plugs and spoons work so well.

Unlike fly patterns that can be reproduced ad infinitum, tyee lures are one-of-a-kind pieces of proven art that fish best in specific kinds of water. The preferred tyee plug is called a "Lucky Louie," a piece of wood or plastic, painted white and shaped like a Conehead larva. The preferred Lucky Louie is called a "plastic Shovel-nose," a 1950s design whose dished-out face really rocks in a strong current. These days, a vintage Shovel-nose can easily go for $350, especially if it has salmon tooth graffiti all over it.

The oldest tyee lure is the spoon, a six or seven-inch piece of bent metal with a silver, chrome, nickel, copper, or brass finish. It is designed to wobble and flash like a wounded herring, especially in sunny weather. By far the favored spoon of the Tyee Pool is British Columbia's own remarkable Gibbs Stewart.

The best tyee tackle is as old as your average baby boomer. Many have names: "The White Witch," for instance (a silver-plated spoon), "Uncle Dick" (a Shovel-nose), "Bland" (a very pale Shovel-nose), "Blue Rhonda" (a Lucky Louie supposedly named after a sexual fantasy), or "The Juggler" (another Shovel-nose and a gift from Paul Magid, a Flying Karamazov Brother with a serious fishing habit).

Tyee guides consider all this hallowed hardware their most prized possession. They guard their plugs and spoons like gold, trade them like stock, and give them to each other for wedding presents. They are heroically generous in loaning them to their clients, but God help the witless angler who loses one — the guilt alone will mess up your concentration for days.

At the moment, we were fishing Rich's hottest plug, a plastic Shovel-nose named "Jesus Murphy" after what Rich said when Scott Laird, one of the Tyee Pool's hottest guides, gave it to him for his birthday. My job was to focus Buddha-like attention on my rod tip while it telegraphed the subaquatic activity of my lure which, under normal conditions, rides the currents of the Tyee Pool like a waltzing heartbeat. But this extra-weird wave action was making Jesus Murphy hip-hop all over the place. If a tyee hit it, I'd be the last to know, especially since the morning was still roughly the color of the interior of a whale, and I couldn't see a damn thing. The storm was still so bad that Rich, who is 6' 6" and has guided in The Pool for twenty years, was having trouble just keeping Lucky from doing another 180. He had to row directly into the wind in order to maintain any position at all, which gets especially complicated when you consider that rowboats go backwards to begin with. The only thing that made any sense that morning was Taj Mahal's grits-and-catfish voice blowing blue smoke out of my pink boom box which we had crammed into a Hefty Bag for the occasion, an appointment that surely would have mortified the Tyee Pool's earliest celebrity, Zane Grey.

A veteran of California's famous Tuna Club of Catalina Island, in 1919 Grey set out to prove that these jumbo salmon could be taken with light tackle, a method that had recently been pioneered for tuna fishing. Thus, he produced a rod with an astonishing six-ounce tip and a reel with wimpy nine-thread line, not the then standard twenty-one.

"How long will this hold a tyee?" Grey asked an Indian guide named Jim.

"About two minutes," Jim replied. Grey hired him on the spot.

Zane Grey's methods turned out to be so successful that light tackle became one of the Tyee Club's hallmarks. But it wasn't he who helped found the Club. It was his favorite fishing buddy, a man who appears in many Zane Grey fishing stories simply as "Lone Angler." Five years after Grey discovered the Tyee Pool, Lone Angler and two other committed Campbell River salmon fishermen decreed right there on the banks of the Tyee Pool that the Club's rules would "do everything possible to conserve for all time the fine run of this outstanding species of salmon."

At the moment, The Cannibal was doing a real decent job of it all by his unholy self. Stiletto torrents assaulted our Helly Hansen rain gear from all directions while Rich cranked like an athlete on the oars.

"Oh, I wish I were an Oscar Meyer wiener!" he sang in his fine sailor's baritone, "Because then I'd be at a picnic instead of rowing this frigging bo-o-oat."

He wasn't the only one. All around us, tyee guides wrestled with the storm while their boats' red and green running lights jumped in the blackness like Christmas-in-a-blender. Normally, predawn tyee fishing is a balm, the water a gel, and the only sound that breaks the quiet is the dull chant of the oars and the occasional watery burst and descending slap of a leaping salmon. But in this storm's noisy chaos, the one force that galvanized us all was the anticipation of The Moment, which would, we knew, soon be upon us — we just didn't know exactly when. Because you never do.

Trout fishing has its morning and evening bites. These are fairly regular events which have to do with the circadian rhythm of insects, the natural feeding cycles of fish, and an angler's innate glee in vexing his or her spouse. But the only thing remotely predictable about tyee fishing is that almost every morning, usually just before or just after or even an hour after dawn, all of a sudden, for no good reason, the fish decide to go for it. Bam! One hits a line five boats to the north. Bam! Bambambam! Another hits two boats due west, and two more hit the two boats off your stern, then a reel sings right behind you. This is The Moment you've been waiting for.

Unfortunately, this is also the moment your mind decided to take a powder. You were thinking about breakfast. You were thinking about sex (this *is* spawning water.) You were thinking about *anything* but the invisible tip of your rod. Shut up. Pay attention. Any moment could be The Moment, you idiot. Then the gold ribbon of sunrise gift wraps the shark-tooth skyline of Quadra Island directly to the east of you, and the morning goes pink. First Light. You are fishing now in the thinnest of air under a sky like bleached opals in water like grape jelly. Finally, you can see. The Cannibal backs off a little, the ice pick rain turns to soft needles, and you note that the tip of your rod is, in fact, nodding away like Ray Charles.

There is a flotilla of twenty-five rowboats in The Pool now. Everyone staring at the rod tip. Everyone quiet. Everyone cold and wet as a clam. Somewhere behind you a seaplane takes off, and in that hanging drone your mind finally implodes. Sound unites. Boundaries blur. Waterskyboatfishguide. You're gone. And that's when The Moment happens, always. The problem is, it usually doesn't happen to you. Tyee are gifts not given lightly. Or often. And of the five or so tyee that may hit that morning, perhaps three will make it to the boat without breaking off — that's the built-in conservation ethic of tyee fishing. And that's why you put in your rod hours, summer after summer after summer.

In September of 1988, the gift of a tyee almost was mine. It was a strange morning, not because of the weather but because the Northern Lights were glowering a Kryptonite green on the northeastern arc of the horizon. In their otherworldly light, Rich took on definite Jolly Green Giant proportions. He was the manager of April Point Lodge back then, the naturalistic, luxury resort whose owners had, since it opened in 1944, steadfastly upheld the tenets of the Tyee Club. They had also generously agreed to let Rich guide me in the Pool that day.

The Tyee Pool is ancient tribal fishing water. When it is quiet it is quiet as a church, and just as sanctified. Maybe more. Residing like it does in that physical limbo between solid and gas, Tyee Pool water feels charged with the possibilities of birth fluid, the creative force liquefied, purified, and able to deliver whole beings as fecund and alive as the electric medium that births them. Because of this, I always do a little ceremony before I go fishing there. That morning I even tried to light a few candles, but they kept blowing out in the wind. Then I tossed a handful of homemade cedar and dill fish offering mixture into the water, most of which flew back in my face. Finally, Rich stood up in the boat and held a tube of Italian anchovy paste above his head, which, given his height, was about Michael Jordan stuff-level, and squished some in each of the cardinal directions while requesting the blessings of the Cannibal at the North End of the World, the Tlingit Indians' Salmon Woman who lives at the head of every salmon stream, and ABC's Curt Gowdy, just to be on the safe side — all to the great amusement of the advertising staff of *Field and Stream* magazine who happened to be standing on the dock at the time because they were on a company retreat at April Point Lodge that week.

Discovery Passage had a good shark-fin chop on it, so Rich and I had towed Lucky-the-Lucky-Rowboat across behind a Boston Whaler which we anchored close to shore in the Potlatch area of the Tyee Pool. By the time we climbed into Lucky the water had flattened out nicely. Its cool skin seemed to produce the little wind that kept playing with our hair. And, again, I felt my body respond to the maternal flood upon which our rowboat was suspended.

The Northern Lights did their strange green polka as I tossed Rich's even stranger Glass-Eyed Stubby Louie overboard, a shorter, pregnant-looking version of your normal Shovel-nose. "Pregnant and Italian," Rich corrected. "Thirteen pulls," he added, and my line went out, glowing in the green light like creme de menthe spider web.

"Weird," I thought. But I felt lucky. It was a layered sensation that feels happy on top and deeply connected to some kind of secret reservoir of preordained good fortune underneath. When the pink snake of morning crawled across the eastern sky it was as if Salmon Woman herself had cast a glamour over everything, a metallic wash that made the water and the air, the mountains, even the pulp mill to the north glitter with the mysterious gleam of living salmon skin that vanishes as soon as the fish leaves the water. I couldn't stand it any longer.

"I feel lucky," I said out loud.

"Me too," Rich replied.

Before the Stubby Louie could nod in agreement, a fish hit it so hard I had no choice but to wake up and smell the coffee that I had just spilled all over my boots.

"We're goin' downtown!" Rich crooned and began rowing for all he was worth. Fortunately, I had hit the rod as hard as the fish had hit Rich's Lucky Louie, so it was seriously hooked. To this day Rich calls my reaction "some kind of ethereal instinct."

The rest was the eternal tango of fisherman and fish. If you happen to have a grand slam salmon on your line, however, the first thing it's going to do is run for all its worth. Let it. You have to let it. Because a spawning tyee that size possesses a locomotive power unlike any other you're likely to encounter, especially on light tackle. And if you *don't* let it run, it will simply snap your line like so much raw spaghetti, a heartbreak even Zane Grey learned the hard way.

My own reel had shrieked like a bagpipe playing "Amazing Grace" in fast forward. All I could do was keep my fingers away from its knuckle buster handles and commence the sport's hymn-like call-and-response. The fish ran fast and I let it, keeping my rod tip up and my line taut at all times because a slack line is an open invitation to a thrown hook. Then, when I felt the slightest pause in the salmon's flight, I reeled in hard, praying it wasn't one of the Tyee Pool's intellectual warriors who turns suddenly and runs toward the boat, making your line go so slack so fast you can expect to reel in an empty hook.

The fish took another long run, shattering the vitreous surface of The Pool this time and presenting its silveriness to the born-again sky. Rich was convinced it was at least a thirty-pounder, and my heart soared.

Thus I played the fish. Run, reel in, run, reel in, and finally, when it tired, reel-reel-reel, all the way home. After thirty minutes of battle, biceps burning way beyond the Jane Fonda comfort zone, I carefully maneuvered the fish to Lucky's starboard side, and Rich netted it perfectly.

Then there was the Second Moment. The one no one likes to talk about. The moment your glorious opponent lies panting at your feet, longer and heavier than your leg, out of its element and out of air, and you are supposed to be very happy. While your guide reaches for his club, you watch in sorrow as that indescribable salmon-shine fades from your fish's opalescent flank — a patina as elegant and blue as the sacred water that produced it, an ancient brilliance replaced in seconds by a haze as dull and gray as the smoke from the upstream mill that often ruins the morning sky. "Steady," you think. "Remember, the run is not endangered and you eat fish. And this is the most honorable way to stock your larder."

Rich gave the beast a single expert lethal blow, and I thought of the little Kalahari Bushman in "The Gods Must Be Crazy," kneeling beside his fallen antelope, hand on horn, explaining that his people needed meat and thanking it for letting them have it. Then there was the somewhat embarrassing question of whether or not this fish would get me into the Tyee Club, which Rich, upon close inspection, was beginning to doubt.

Sure enough, it was a pound and a half light. But it was a male and most certainly a thing of beauty. Even in death, his colors failing, his geometry was stunning. The line from his nose to his dorsal fin ran ruler straight, giving him a profile more like a Roman god's than a fish's. He was built to swim like a torpedo, so suited to that icy salmon race track that he looked like congealed water, not flesh, fin, and bone.

Back at the lodge, Eiji San, April Point's official Japanese fish print maker, pronounced him the most beautiful salmon he'd ever seen. The print still hangs proudly above my desk. The *Field and Stream* guys were pretty impressed, too. A number of them had their picture taken with me and my fish, then, somehow, just with my fish. And at dinner, several of them approached me individually and whispered, "Do you, ah, have any of that fish offering stuff left?"

Rich's and my first fish didn't get me into the Tyee Club, and we haven't landed another salmon since. There just aren't as many mammoth tyee as there used to be. The magnificent Campbell River chinook run crashed in the early '80s due to pollution from an upstream copper mine. A hatchery program managed to save the original genetic material, but the gravel of the tributary where it was built isn't anywhere near the size of the Campbell's. Thus a smaller, more environmentally appropriate strain of salmon is replacing the titan tyee that thrilled light-tackle anglers for nearly a hundred years.

But the Tyee Pool still produces a fifty-pounder from time to time. And so I go. Summer after summer, year after year, sitting dutifully in Lucky while Rich works the oars on mornings the color of eels, in water like a melted sunrise, that ever startling, transitional medium between air and land that has for so long been mankind's earthly linkage, God's divine filler. And holding my tyee rod with hands like frozen squid while my mascara runs like squid ink, I wait again for the moment that Rich's Shovel-nose Louie dances one too many times down the Tyee Pool and a monster of a Pacific chinook goes ballistic and I finally fish my way into the Tyee Club of British Columbia while the champagne water of Discovery Passage says to the beautiful black sky, "Throw your big leg up over me, mama, I might never feel this good again."

Lana Janine Born Again

Joan Skogan

SCENE 1: DECK OF *LANA JANINE*, GOLETAS CHANNEL, MORNING

NARRATOR:

Goletas Channel is the beginning of black cod fishing. Southeast wind and my teeth are clenched on remembered beach forts made from seaworn planks; on footprints across flat, damp sand; on arbutus trees and uncontrollably green salal that signal the limit of the sea's reach. My icons of the warm-blooded earth cannot help me now — my desk, my mother, my black silk dress are not here at Nahwitti Bar. Only the wooden hull of *Lana Janine*, formerly named *Mary Lou*, is between me and the sea.

MUSIC: HELLO MARY LOU, GOODBYE HEART

NARRATOR:

Thirty-two hours northwest of Nahwitti Bar is Bowie Seamount, 1,200 fathoms deep, almost 200 sea miles offshore. Black cod country.

ENGINEER:

Bowie ain't the end of the world. (PAUSE) But you can see the end of the world from here.

DECKHAND:

Holy fuck, that buoy line…

CAPTAIN:

I spend so goddamn much time out here, I'm going to get me a post office box labelled 53 degrees 18 minutes north, 135 degrees west.

NARRATOR:

First time I step into *Lana's* wheelhouse, I'm six years old again in Herbert Spencer school in New Westminster. Wet hardwood and something else smells the same.

COOK:

Don't need no marine weather report. We got wind, wave, and swell height right here in the galley since her whole cabin shifted in the blow last winter coming across the Sound.

CAPTAIN:

Liftin' that black cod trap's harder than holding a racing form, eh? Did you just wake up and figure out you're not still back in town?

DECKHAND:

You need Helly Hansen rain pants lessons, woman? Keep *both* straps in your right hand while you climb in. Bring them over your right shoulder together, yeah.

COOK:

Ain't none of you wearing rain gear in this galley. Not over your knees anyhow.

SCENE 2: DECK OF *LANA JANINE*, BOWIE SEAMOUNT, NIGHT

NARRATOR:

Eleven P.M. and still day. There's light on the edge of the sky all night, or maybe this is morning. We are not sure any more on *Lana Janine*. We stand on her tilting deck, our hands tucked inside the bibs of our rain pants and stare down into the sea or out into the sky. Sister Anne, Sister Anne, I want to call to the emptiness offshore. Is there anyone coming? Anyone speeding across the plain of the sea toward us? No. No one is coming. No one is out here but us.

CAPTAIN:

No fuckin' dinner until two fuckin' A.M. when the fuckin' fish are in the fuckin' freezers.

COOK:

We're having roast beef, mashed potatoes, gravy, asparagus, corn, white buns, green salad, and fruit salad.

ENGINEER:

Stove's a goddamn foundry. Supposed to come out of the old penitentiary. Probably they sentenced prisoners to cook on it. Or be baked in it. Stove's probably as old as *Lana* herself.

DECKHAND:

This guy escapes from jail, eh. He's on the run and he stows away on a black cod boat, then when they go in to deliver, he runs up the dock fast as he can go, yelling for the cops, and gives himself up. Guy begs to go back to jail instead of out on the black cod.

CAPTAIN:

Run up top, will you, woman, and snap that switch marked "daylight." We could use some down here.

ENGINEER:

Albatrosses are drowned halibut fishermen. Their spirits.

DECKHAND:

I saw this guy come out of his wheelhouse two seasons back with an M-16 and shoot an albatross. He pikes it out of the water, plucks it, sticks it in the oven, eats one bite, and chucks it overboard.

CAPTAIN:

The guy who runs *Lana* when I'm in town, he'll just tell you, "plenty of good men left on shore," if you complain about anything out here. Bitch any more and he'll give you a Norwegian wheel turn. Six hours on and stay on.

NARRATOR:

...winds north to northwest rising overnight. Seas three to four meters late afternoon. *Lana Janine*, half full of black cod, is still rolling.

She cannot stop herself. The heavy mast which held her steady has been removed to make room for more black cod gear. Now she rolls without ceasing, her motion a part of her and now a part of us.

CAPTAIN:

SNOW PASS LANA JANINE. SNOW PASS LANA JANINE. VIKING PRIDE LANA JANINE. NEPTUNE 11 LANA JANINE. This goddamn radio doesn't put out worth a goddamn. I can hear them like they was down in the galley and they're how many hundred miles south, but can they pick me up?

ENGINEER:

I keep dreaming I'm down under the keel looking at her zincs.

COOK:

So when he gets back to town there's nothing left but the curtains waving in the wind. She took everything else.

CAPTAIN:

Pass me that Strawberry Quik. I didn't know they still made it.

ENGINEER:

One of the pumps down there's labelled "1943." How they think I can...The main engine's Caterpillar and the starboard auxiliary's a Cummins, so they'll be turning over when the rest of her's...

DECKHAND:

Big Boat Joe, now, he's still on the salmon with...

COOK:

That's the guy they call Boomchain.

CAPTAIN:

So he calls home from Bella Bella. She answers and he's real mad, says, "Where the fuck are you?" She screams, "I answered the phone, didn't I?"

NARRATOR:

I dreamed I was in Regina and the city was a garden with grassy paths and roses.

COOK:

He never pays up in Vegas, eh, just goes home to Vancouver and starts drinking. Sunday night, two big guys are at his door, looking for their money. They say they don't have Monday on their calendar. He had to wake up the money boys at B.C. Packers, get somebody out of bed to give the Vegas guys next year's fishing check.

ENGINEER:

The other guy who runs *Lana*, he's Norwegian, so if the gear snags on the bottom, he'll throw a sugar lump into the sea. She wants something sweet, he says. Sometimes it works.

NARRATOR:

The deck rail outside my cabin is broken away. I figure if I open my door and step out while we're rolling down to port, I'll skitter across the deck and run right into the sea.

ENGINEER:

The Japanese fishermen say there's ghosts in Christie Pass at that place by Scarlett Point where the grass always looks like it's just been cut.

CAPTAIN:

I was still crewing on this other boat then. We were outside Gowgaia and it was the worst I've ever known. The old man and his two boys are up the wheelhouse with their survival suits on, screaming at us to shift the traps on the deck, get some balance back on her. We're slanted over pretty bad. This young kid, his first trip, he starts crying. "We're going to die, we're going to die," he says over and over, then he starts to scream it out. I had to hit him. "Snap out of it," I tell him. "We need you to help move this fucking gear if we're not going to die." We get the traps shifted and get into Gowgaia Bay somehow. I see that kid sometimes when we deliver in Port Hardy. He won't even come onto the dock. He's happy driving the ore truck for Utah Mines.

SCENE 3: DECK OF *LANA JANINE*, FRASER RIVER ENTRANCE, MORNING

NARRATOR:

Thirty-two days fishing and running time to Bowie Seamount. Fifty hours south, the open ocean and Bowie are far behind us. *Lana Janine* is moving slowly; loaded with black cod and settling low in the fresh water of the Fraser River. In the north arm of the river, she is regarded briefly, incuriously, by drivers on the Knight Street bridge as she backs awkwardly into the Northsea unloading dock.

SCENE 4: VANCOUVER

NARRATOR:

A fisherman at the race track says the man who owned *Lana* when she was still *Mary Lou*, and still had her mast, is dead. No, says this old halibut fisherman on Hastings Street, just drinking all the time is all.

OLD MAN:

I loved my first boat, but not her. Not *Mary Lou*. I was afraid of her. Everything I had, including my wife, was paid for until I went out and got her. *Mary Lou's* fuel tanks are in the bow, so she ploughed the water, and that slanted stern made her a pig in a following sea. You say they've taken her mast off. She'd roll like a whore.

MUSIC: HELLO MARY LOU, GOODBYE HEART

NARRATOR:

When *Lana Janine* aka *Mary Lou* burned and sank off Gowgaia Bay on the west coast of the Charlottes on March 18, 1992, I was in the Yukon, telling stories to school kids about black cod fishing and other voyages. The man who gave me the news when I returned to the coast said her crew got off, but I fought with him anyway. He made so little of her loss. He didn't know her at all.

Last night I dreamed I was back on the *Lana Janine*, diving again and again from her deck into the deep water offshore, searching for some unnamed treasure I had lost. The water was cloudy, not clear as it is on Bowie Seamount, where you see dolphins and porpoises flying along the keel fathoms down. Sometimes I became disoriented, swimming further down, thinking I was making my way toward air and light.

Above me, the captain and crew stood on *Lana's* deck again. The engineer, the cook, and the deckhands were not much interested in my underwater search, but each man carefully minded the lines and the gear so the boat would stay in position for me. I continued to look below for the nameless, lost treasure, while on the surface *Lana Janine* had ceased her constant trembling roll and moved easily on a quiet sea.

Learning to Love Sea Level

@@@

Rick Rubin

Call me a serial-mass-drowner. In 1983 and 1984 I drowned the four principal cities of the United States West Coast, and contemplated drowning a fifth, (it was San Diego, but I spared it). I offered my services to certain East Coast interests to drown their cities as well. I supplied carefully devised maps showing the extent of the devastation.

The first map showed sea level about twenty feet higher, after the West Antarctic Ice Sheet got its feet wet and dissolved. The West Antarctic Ice Sheet was the supposed culprit because its base is below present sea level. Should the water warm and rise, the ice sheet might go pretty quickly, and it's total meltdown would raise the level of the world's seas by approximately nineteen feet. Many scientists suppose that the melting might slow to a dribble at that time. Other scientists concede the possibility of losing Greenland's ice cap as well. A mere twenty feet would flood out most of the docks in the world and low lying areas anywhere near water. For example, Bangladesh.

The second map showed the waters maxed out three hundred feet above present sea level, after all the glaciers of earth had melted. The three hundred foot scenario was a delight so rare that I mapped it for the entire West Coast.

South Los Angeles and Long Beach were drowned all the way to Whittier. A wide bay appeared from Santa Monica to just north of

Laguna Beach, with big Palo Verde Island offshore and a few smaller knobs still rising above the powder-blue sea. The California central valleys, Sacramento and San Joaquin, filled up like big watering troughs from almost Bakersfield to nearly Red Bluff, with Sutter Buttes Island towering jagged above the placid inland sea.

At three hundred feet of water, downtown Seattle was gone and Puget Sound rearranged, a number of islands having sunk beneath the greatly widened inland sea and new ones created. The Sound now opened to the sea at Grays Harbor as well as Port Angeles, making the Olympic Peninsula an island. Puget Bay extended almost to the Columbia River but didn't quite crest the low hills north of the Cowlitz River valley.

The Columbia had become a saltwater fjord to where it splashed a considerable distance up the face of McNary Dam, two hundred ninety-two miles from the present mouth of the river. Portland's downtown was entirely immersed, only scattered settlements surviving on the hills, where goat-herds roam and fishermen put out to fish among the Portland high-rises. The Willamette Valley had become Willamette Sound, which extended to Harrisburg, fifteen miles south of Eugene. Should the low pass to Puget Bay be drowned, or a canal dug, it would connect Harrisburg, Oregon, with the Inside Passage to Alaska.

I did not cease my drowning with the inundation of a scatter of coastal geography on this far shore. I delighted in mapping new bays and fjord-like extensions of the sea, the overtopping of multimillion dollar docks and shipyards, the inexorable destruction of the proud towers and parking structures along every seacoast and in some places far inland. I postulated that the word "Holland" would come to mean a total wipe-out, a position not to get yourself into, after the sea took that lowland nation back. As in, "Don't Holland me, baby." I imagined a scenario where most of the seacoast cities would bankrupt themselves building vast systems of dikes, which would give them a few decades of life, but as the pace quickened and the waters rose more swiftly, the inevitable trudge up into the hills by impoverished humans would continue.

I utterly obliterated vast reaches of India, savaged northern Russia and Siberia with my waters, and drowned the entire centers of Africa and South America. It was breathtaking and habit forming to discover such vast changes from a mere increase in how much free water there is on Earth.

The Oregonian's Sunday magazine *Northwest*, where I published the first of what I came to think of as "the Glub series," buried my story in mid-magazine. I think the editor was sorry later, after I went out of my way to show him the other magazines, as they appeared, featuring it as their cover story. The cover of the *San Francisco Examiner's* Sunday magazine *California Living*, for example, showed the Transamerica pyramid paunch deep and alone in a cerulean sea, a motorboat speeding past. Their maps were better drawn than the ones I'd sent them. The cover of the *Los Angeles Daily News* Sunday magazine showed waves and a mean chop battering a downtown L.A. thick with buildings that Los Angelenos would no doubt recognize. They used the maps I sent, one of all California and a close-up of the L.A. Basin. The *Seattle Weekly* cover art showed a drowned Space Noodle.

I found it interesting that nobody Back East showed the slightest interest in having me drown their cities for them. I would cheerfully have drowned New York, where I spent a year in slummy agony, or Boston, where I spent a summer. It wouldn't have been hard; contour maps were my secret, and the public library has lots. Unless I knew the city a little, it was just words, without local color and humor, so I never drown any place I haven't lived in or visited hard. I figure those East Coast editors simply aren't in touch with their environment enough to want to have it drowned.

This was early for popular stories about the Greenhouse and its effects. I published my first one in November, 1983. Carl Sagan didn't get in on the rising sea level until February, 1985 — almost a year-and-a-half later. His *Parade Magazine* story had a great illustration, also showing a drowned San Francisco, but the story covered the disintegration of the Antarctic Ice Sheet in an offhand, almost disrespectful manner. He talked a lot about gasses.

By contrast, I went for drama. I predicted the event for the year 2014. Maybe I fudged a little there. Everybody gets a bit wild at times, especially for a good cause. Or a good lead sentence. But scientists can be just as speculative. I found one scientist who suggested that the meltdown might cause the earth to wobble on its axis, and a 1970s study which found that the ocean had risen three inches in only eight years. That pencils out to about three feet a century.

What lent a certain immediacy to my speculations was fact: The process of sea level change has been going on for a lot longer than most people realize. During the centuries while the Ice Age glaciers were melting, sea level rose fairly swiftly. Ice Age mean low tide was about three hundred feet below today's. Perhaps the rise averaged three feet a century over a period of ten thousand years.

Then sea level steadied. For the past three thousand years the seas have risen a piddling four inches a century, about ten feet during the entire period. Emergent mankind was lulled. But now all that may be changing, according to some scientists. The sea rose six inches during the past century and is expected to rise twenty-eight inches during the next one. We may be wading about at the very median of postglacial sea levels, and the total rise may reach fully six hundred feet. So much for beach front properties as a long term investment.

It may have happened more than once. The water level in Bathtub Earth has been veering wildly (in geological time, of course) ever since the beginnings of the oceans themselves. Naturally, from a human standpoint there was generally time to load your knickknacks, bundle up the kids, and hike up to the next higher flat place inland. But if you lived on an exposed coast, the coming of the floods might be heralded by a freak storm timed just wrong.

For example, to destroy Los Angeles I arranged:

"Just as a record winter snowpack began to melt off, one of the most unusual storms in the history of Southern California came roaring up out of the Southwest. The wind-pushed sea rose to the equivalent of a twenty-one-foot tide. The Los Angeles, San Gabriel, and Santa Ana rivers, blocked by the Pacific Ocean near their mouths, overflowed for the first time in many decades."

In the depth of the Ice Age, when the sea was three hundred feet lower, the rivers ran down deep troughs carved into bedrock, and the shore was out around the edge of the continental shelf. We're talking a snap of our geological fingers here, not more than fifteen or twenty centuries ago. The beds of tidewater rivers have filled with sand or silt since, covering all traces of the crime, but the canyons lurk beneath.

One hundred and twenty-five thousand years ago sea level rose to a higher level than today. Like a snowman in a puddle, once it started, the West Australian Ice Sheet must have gone all the way. At least that's what some scientists think. One scientist pointed out that the earth was between ice ages a hundred and twenty-five thousand years ago, and the world's temperature then was as high as it is today. We're between Ice Ages too, though our temperature is rising for other reasons, or so some scientists believe.

Not that a total meltdown should necessarily be viewed as an unmitigated evil. Isaac Asimov figured that without the glaciers there would be less land but fewer deserts, because it would rain more. Winds would decrease, since the rise in temperature at the poles would temper the contrast between tropics and Arctics, which has always caused an enormous convection current, rising hot from the tropics, descending cold upon the poles. Without that great planetary wind, the tropics will warm a little but the poles will warm a lot. Asimov's calculations suggested the three hundred feet above present sea level figure too, but he supposed the additional weight might push down the lowlands and ocean floors, so the rise in tide would be a mere two hundred feet.

Drowned cities, though hazards to navigation, and even less good for real estate interests, will be happy hunting grounds for generations of scuba-diving anthropologists, and reefs of unprecedented richness, to the great joy of the fish. Mississippi Bay will extend clear to Southern Illinois, the romantic tidewater south will feed mackerel from Brownsville, Texas, to Norfolk, Virginia; the wine-dark Atlantic will extend up the Hudson Valley and inundate the St. Lawrence River clear to Lake Ontario, almost but not quite cutting off New England and New Brunswick from the continent.

Consider as well the entertainment value for those of us smart enough (or lucky enough) to live above the future high tide. The potential for a good-old-fashioned slow-motion disaster exists.

Let me postulate a sequence of events. First a flood, then the next flood and the beginning of the first dikes. Feverish efforts ensue. The federal government moves to Wilkes Barre, D.C., and thirty-six-foot tides are reported. A new mean sea level is declared but that doesn't fool anyone for long. After a while a great public apathy sets in, based on the curious notion that the sea is inexorable and its waves cannot be stopped. Indeed, some noted theologians argue this position, while ministers of the gospel preach that we can hope for divine intervention in the near future, if only we all pray real hard and tithe. Scientists issue grim pronouncements but continue to apply for grants to solve the problem of the rising sea.

In the next stage a national crusade is raved into being by politico-babble and the daily press. High-tech dikes are built across every exposed area of the nation, a program that dwarfs into insignificance the Great Wall of China. The bankrupt federal government is in Denver, D.C. San Francisco consists of seven charming islands, each one occupied by persons of a different race or sex. Everyone and everything is flat broke. Yet still the water doeth rise.

The center of Australia and the basins of the Congo, Amazon, Yangtse, and Ganges are under water. Northern Canada and Northern Asia rejoin the Arctic Ocean. Cairo, Illinois, is the great seaport of Middle America, where deep draft ocean freighters tie up to the moveable floating docks that have become so popular with port authorities. The water sloshes across the twenty-first floor of the World Trade towers in Manhattan, and winter storms splash higher still. Much of northern Europe has disappeared, Greenland is showing actual green and southeast Asia is a string of charming islands almost to Chiang Mai in northern Thailand.

Buy land at the three-hundred-foot level, I counsel you, my readers. Build a dock there, and dangle your dory off the end. Don't worry if your neighbors laugh at you, just wait. Remember: coastal land has always commanded a premium. Learn to love sea level! Trust me; it will stop at three hundred feet. And prices for shoreline property futures have never been lower.

Baptism

Lorian Hemingway

Outside the paper mill town of Pine Bluff, the Arkansas River spreads out broad like a plain, meeting up with young boys gone for a summer swim, and swallows them whole without ever asking their names. It is the river from my childhood, clouded by red clay, steady and deep, its current forceful as an avalanche. In spring when the floods came I would watch the river from the safety of the high, sandbagged levee, its dark water clogged with mangled car parts, whole trunks of trees uprooted by tornadoes, and tangled fists of rusted barbed wire. It was a seasonal ritual in Pine Bluff, watching the gruesome bounty of the floods, and I was as shameless as any in my curiosity.

    I saw the body of a young girl once, flying in that water, her thin blond hair matted with twigs and reddish foam that churned in the wake of the surge as she slid down the chute of the river, far from where she'd started out, far from the calm of that spring morning before the storms came. Her eyes were wide-open like two cat's-eye marbles, and the skin around her mouth was as blue and transparent as oiled paper. I remember understanding in that instant of seeing her — a girl, my own age, dead — the unchecked power of the water that bore her up. And I understood then that a river could murder, randomly, with no thought given to the lives it pulled into its fury.

    I used to think a lot about that girl, imagine where she'd lived, what she'd been like, why she'd ended up as a broken, dirty doll flying past my high perch on the levee. I told myself she had wanted to swim in the waist-high flood that spring, be carried, weightless, by the current into some new place she'd yet to see. Every kid wanted to ride the floods but few were allowed. She was the one who had dared to do it, ignoring her mother's warnings. She'd swum into a whirlpool and couldn't get out. A tree branch or an old car part had clobbered her. She'd been knocked unconscious, then drowned. I dreamt about her for awhile, and in my dreams she'd always come to life just as she bobbed past, raise her head up out of the blood-colored water, and call to me, "It's O.K. Come on in," and I'd turn my head quickly in the dream, remembering the glassed-over eyes of the real girl, afraid if I stared too long she'd seize my hand and pull me into the spinning water.

For a long time I feared death by water, yet summer after summer I still made treks to the clay banks below the levee, usually with my aunt Freda. We'd spend our afternoons pushing worm-rigged cane poles into the muddy water of the Arkansas, sunbathing in the humid mornings before the mosquitoes settled in, thick as a fog. I ate great handfuls of the river on particularly idle days, tempted by the potent scent of minerals in the red clay, and smeared what I didn't eat on my body, watching it dry orange in the sun, so tight on my skin it cracked and fell off in chunks as I ran into the water.

Freda was often my only companion during those summers that could last from March until October, a half-Cherokee woman raised in a Catholic orphanage who later became a Carmilite nun, and later still gave up the order and the church entirely for full-time exploration into the theories of Carl Jung. She was Pine Bluff's token eccentric — many called her crazy — whose physical beauty was matched only by her complete disregard for conventional thought. I was her student in summer, a refugee from Mississippi, beguiled by her beauty, completely willing to sit at her feet on the sun-baked clay, listening.

Freda told me that the Arkansas, as red sometimes as leaves in Indian summer, was very like the blood of Christ itself, capable of healing and life-sustaining grace, a benefactor, in a way, to those who availed themselves of its power. This notion went contrary to the cold-blooded slaughter I had witnessed in these waters just a few summers before, and I suspected that Freda was, perhaps, as crazy as people said. I'd sit quietly, staring up at her as she talked, my eyes wide, as she agreeably allowed me to stuff my cheeks with mud, thinking, I imagine now, that I was merely indulging a sacrament.

We took a picnic basket to a grove of cottonwoods along the riverbank one Sunday morning, Freda and I, in the summer of my fifteenth year. It was clear and hot already, and I could smell the clay damp along the banks from dew that had settled. It smelled like the ravine behind my mother's house in Mississippi, wet earth and minerals so potent my mouth watered when I breathed deep.

As she started out across the river, Freda was drinking ice water from a fruit jar. I was spread out on the blanket we had brought, eating a meatball sandwich, one of Freda's specialities. She wasted nothing. When the sauce was gone, out of the pot came the meatballs. She'd crumble them up on eggs or mix them with the fried okra; this morning they'd been sliced dry onto two pieces of Sunbeam bread, the kind you can mash into a ball, throw at the ceiling, and have it stick.

Freda turned around to look at me, smoothing out the blanket, something her mother had given her, all orange and green and purple in a crazy pattern.

"You hear that?" Freda asked me, turning away quickly.

"Hear what?" I asked.

"Listen."

I listened, thinking maybe it was the river noises.

"I don't hear anything," I said. "What am I supposed to be hearing?"

"That," she said impatiently, moving her arms out in a direction upriver from us.

There was no wind and sounds came up on you suddenly. I could hear something now, the way you do when a radio knob is turned up slowly, the music coming closer and then nearly filling my head. I thought I could feel the ground start to vibrate beneath me.

"What is it?" I asked, excited.

"Sssh. Quiet," Freda said.

I had heard the sound before, rising up on a Saturday night from the tiny church that fronted the alley behind Freda's house. It was a gospel song — not a hymn, slow and reverent — and the voices yelled at full timbre and harmonized, Glory! Glories! It grew stronger and stronger, moving through the cottonwoods with such force I saw birds scatter from the trees. When I listened to that chorus of voices from my bed at Freda's, I'd be covered in goose flesh, the hair on the back of my neck pricking up, throbbing with the pulse of the music.

"Here they come," Freda said, pointing in the same direction, "right through the trees."

I looked down at my arms and watched the skin rise up. I saw them then, a whole congregation of black people, maybe two hundred, coming down the bank through the cottonwoods, their long robes trailing across the red clay until they looked as if they'd been dipped in blood, their mouths open so wide as they sang I could see the soft pink of tongues and the flashing of gold teeth in the sun.

"Lord Jesus meet us by the river," I heard them sing in full-bellowed voices, not one timid note among them.

> *"Wash us in the blood,*
> *in the blood*
> *oh the blood, dear Jesus,*
> *of the lamb."*

Several called out "Hallelujah" and fell to their knees on the shore.

I looked at Freda and she put a finger to her lips.

"If we're quiet," she whispered, "they won't go away."

The head of the congregation, a big man the color of jet, held his arms up high and spread them wide.

He looked as if he were ready to ascend, his robe blowing back from a wind that had quickly risen. He called out to his people in a deep, full voice, "Brothers and sisters, walk with me now. Let these water re-*leve'e* the sins of this earth. Be saved, in the name of sweet Jesus, by the miracle of the water. By the miracle, children. Let the Lord hear you children, shout Hallelujah, brothers and sisters."

He took a breath, his arms still raised high, and I could see his chest swell beneath the robe, full as a ten-year oak.

"Into the water, sisters, into the water now, brothers. Cleanse your souls shiny white as these robes, white as the light of Jesus.

"Sing Hallelujah, children."

"Hallelujah!" they shouted back, so long and loud I could see the ice in Freda's water jar rattle.

My head was light with the sound of them, Hallelujahs rising in my own throat, choked back and then free again. I wanted to sing with them, thrash on the bank and roll limp into the river. The feeling was so strong I coughed and sputtered until Freda slapped me hard on the back.

They started into the river then, dozens of them, beckoned by the preacher who called out as they passed, "Bless you sister, bless you brother, sweet Jesus, bless you all. Taste the Glory, children. Submerge your souls in the light. Praise Jesus. Hallelujah!"

"Praise Jesus," they sang back. "Praise the Lord."

And the gospel blues pulled them straight toward the water as if they had been born of it.

I watched as their robes billowed up around them, pockets of air caught in the fabric carrying them high over their heads, and then they went down, swaying with the current, one by one, the preacher laying his broad hand atop each head, crying out, "In the name of the everlasting blood of the lamb, I baptize you."

As they went under, their robes caught in the water like dying swans and went down with them. Some held their arms up as they went under, and I thought I could hear a "Praise Jesus" bubble to the surface.

For an instant I moved to stand up, the call in me so strong I had to fight it. We watched them struggle up out of the water, singing as they came onto the bank, their robes heavy now and flattened against their bodies. I noticed some of the women had huge breasts, round as melons beneath the wet fabric, and that the men looked like boys, shy, surrounded by all this womanhood. They sang louder when they were clear of the water, clapping wet hands together and moving like a black and white snake, single file through the trees. In their retreat I could see the women shake their hips in rhythm to the music, and I felt a sweet pain low in my belly. If they had seen us, they had not let on.

I looked down at my arms, at the goose flesh risen up in dark points on this hot summer morning, and wished I had followed them in. I turned to Freda sitting there on the old Indian blanket, her bright, beautiful face lifted high, a peculiar smile on it that made me happy.

"I'm going in," I told her. She nodded as if she already knew.

I didn't sing as I moved down the bank toward the water, looking across to the other side where two young boys fished with cane poles. I didn't know anything to sing except "Honeycomb." But I could still hear them far down the river and imagined I was part of their congregation, about to be made pure and simple, washed free of something whose name I did not yet know. I'd seen their faces when they'd come out, lost in something that brought amazement to their eyes. They were free. Oh yes. I could see it. A miracle had taken place in that water. I swore to myself it was so. I'd seen that same look they'd had, once, in an airport, on the face of a tall black woman. She wore a two-inch-high rhinestone pin on her jacket that read JESUS. I remember reaching out to touch her as I walked past — wanting to touch her — and how she turned around quickly and smiled at me, her eyes patient and understanding, filled with a notion of heaven.

The water felt warm at first, then cooler further out where the bottom started to slip away. I felt a slow panic begin to move in me, starting at my knees, then filling my chest, as I remembered the girl, her arms limp in the river swell. I looked back toward the bank and saw Freda watching me.

"I'll hold my breath," I called out, asking for reassurance.

"I think you should," she called back.

I went down slowly, the thin cotton of my T-shirt turning wet against my breasts.

I stayed down as long as I could, my cheeks puffed out like a guppy's, feeling the current pushing between my outspread legs, my toes gripping the firm river bottom. I felt like a reed in some underwater wind, not sure what I was doing. The water was cool and heavy with the current, and I imagined it was as deep as outer space. I spread my arms out the way the preacher had done, and a thought came into my head so loud and clear my eyes opened in the dark water.

"Help me," it said, over and over, first deep, then high, then meek as a child's plea. "Help me." My mouth opened in surprise and I tasted the rich blood of the water choking me; and the voice grew louder. I imagined the girl there with me, her hand outstretched in the current, fingertips gripping mine, her flesh as warm as the water in which we floated. I imagined, too, the firm hold of her hand as we burst together into the air, our lungs filling in a rush, greedily, our arms held high above our heads.

"You baptized yet," Freda called from the cottonwoods as I walked slowly from the river, falling to the red clay bank, exhausted. I raised my arm and waved my hand once, a signal, yes, and saw for a brief moment the girl there beside me, her hair bright in the warm August sun.

Walking on Water

Ed Edmo

For some reasons a five-year-old can't understand, us Indians were not allowed into the big swimming pool, with its deep greenish-blue water and the high diving boards. If we wanted to get wet at the pool, we had to go to the toddler's wading pool — even grown men and women. I guess the white people believed a little of their white would rub off and we would experience some, but not all, of their privilege.

There was a vicious prejudice against Indians in the small town near the fishing village where I grew up. The stores in The Dalles, Oregon, had signs displayed in the windows stating "NO DOGS OR INDIANS ALLOWED." These signs were in most of the store windows, not just a few stores. Indians were only allowed to eat in one cafe, and that was on the east side of town where the winos, prostitutes, and bootleggers hung out.

One time, the Boy's and Girl's Club had a "Swim Day." My brother was a member, and we were to go to the swimming pool on a Saturday morning. On that Friday night the tension in the kitchen oozed out like the dull light of the coal oil lamp. Mom and Dad talked in hushed voices, and I could see the seriousness in Mom's face. She was straining to get her words out. Dad gestured with his forefinger extended like he hammered nails, and I saw him hammer nails a lot.

When we arrived at the swimming pool, we joined a long line of kids who were members of the club. Behind the counter a young teenage white boy was red-faced mad. Mr. Warren, the flamboyant leader of the

Club, had a receipt in his hand and was waving it in the air like a flag over the top hat he wore on special occasions.

Finally, he phoned the new manager of the pool. Looking back at my brother and me, Mr. Warren said that the Boy's and Girl's Club membership was open to needy children. Well, I had Mom and Dad, and my grandma lived on the hill above me with a warm, welcome wood stove. I didn't think that I was "needy." Sometimes we ran out of food, and then we just went to the missionary's house to eat.

Mr. Warren asked my brother and me when we last took a bath and we both answered, "This morning, sir!" He talked in a hushed tone. After a long time, he handed the phone to the hot-faced boy, who slammed the receiver down. There was a lot of cussing as my brother and I went up to get our baskets. "Dirty Indians!" one of the others said from behind the big desk.

I remember how glad I felt as we peeled off our clothes and put on brand new bathing suits Mom got us from the J.C. Penney. Then we took our showers, not minding the cold water, and marched triumphantly into the "big" swimming pool. I went down to the shallow end and looked at the wide expanse of green-blue, and felt like I could walk on water.

Well, this worked pretty good, going to the swimming pool on hot days. But one time Mom was late picking me up after I got out of the pool. I was standing in the shade by the dressing room, when five white boys came up and taunted me.

"Go back where you belong, savage!"

"Stay in your village, war whoop!"

"We don't want you around here, you dirty Little Indian."

They began pushing me, then grabbed my towel and threw it to the ground, and began hitting and kicking me. I covered myself and swung haymakers at them. A couple of my punches connected, which added to their hostility. When one of the blond boys grabbed my arm and pulled it around behind me and added pressure, I cried out in pain.

Just then my mother drove up with the car horn blaring. The white boys saw her and began running. I tried to run after them but Mom just held me. "Never mind. They've all got small hearts to pick on you."

I wished I had the power to walk on water!

Shapeshifting

Jeffery Smith

When I was four, I stood on a wooden dock and watched my father drop his father into the Ohio River. I remember my Grandpap Smith's bald head bobbing and surfacing like the underbelly of some diseased fish. Even when he was sober — which was seldom — Grandpap couldn't swim; so on that June afternoon thirty years ago, under his customary handicap of a quart or so of Wild Irish Rose wine, Grandpap floundered in the powerful current as my father hovered over the end of the dock, his arms crossed tightly against his chest, and watched silently. His brush cut blonde hair bristled in the late afternoon sun.

On that afternoon, my mother was seven months pregnant, and Grandpap had already advanced several theories meant to convince my dad that the child she carried could not be of his get. He also tried to give me a beer, a project my father did not approve of. I wanted the beer; along with my blue eyes and blonde hair, that settled for Grandpap my own lineage. My mother's people didn't drink, and Grandpap had a genetic theory of his own: "It's a medical fact," he had told my dad, "that if the natural father's got blue eyes his babies can't have nothin' else but blue eyes." And it is a fact that all five of Grandpap's boys had his eyes, identical and unchanging, as blue as robin's eggs.

My dad worked his jaws furiously. I stood between these men, and Grandpap's blue eyes leveled with mine as he sat on the edge of the dock cradling his wine between his legs. My dad pulled from his pocket a foil pouch of Beech-Nut and laid a chaw into his cheek. He stayed silent, watching his fishing line flutter with the breeze. I stared at the current until I wasn't able to tell if it was the water or the dock that moved; maybe the dock carried us along like a floating island, and the river was still.

Grandpap Smith raised one eyebrow. "You mark my words, Bob." He turned broadside and sought my dad's eyes. "That baby, when it comes, it'll look like one a them Black Irish Thomases. That slut's fixin' to put another ring through your nose so you can work your ass off while she's spreadin' 'em for every deadbeat in this county."

My father rose up slowly then, gathered his father into his arms, and dumped him into the river.

The Ohio gurgled and thrashed mightily in those days before it was girdled with dams from Pittsburgh to Cairo. Within a few moments Grandpap had been dragged twenty feet downstream. Just as I wondered what my dad would do, he arced off the dock and into the Ohio. With a few easy and swift strokes he reached Grandpap, hooked him under his arm, and towed his father to shore.

I think now that my dad — who was twenty-two — had realized his inheritance by then, the Smith men's long propensity for violence and rot gut booze. I think he had moved far enough into his father's skin to smell the wound, and recognize it as his own. Maybe my father believed the river water would for once and all scab both wounds, and free him to begin again.

Thirty years later, I came West. When I turned twenty-two, I began to have nightmares about killing my father. I spent the next decade shaping my life with no other guide but to blot those dreams and thin whatever blood I shared with him. I had to find my own shape, move out of his shade, and get as far as I could from those hills and hollers. You can draw a circle on the map, five miles in diameter, with the Ohio at its center, and inside that circle you have nearly all my family, close and distant.

You'd have to extend that circle 2,500 miles to get me inside it now. The Clark Fork that flows behind my house in Missoula is a dozen rivers west of the Ohio, and flows in the opposite direction. I wonder if the waters from Stillhouse Run and Bares Run and Possum Creek — all those streams I chased, as a child, down to their meeting with the Ohio

— still linger in my cells, and will they mingle there with these rivers I call home now — Clark Fork and Blackfoot and Bitterroot — that go to the Pacific?

When we returned home from the dock that June day, my father left without a word. We knew from experience that he wouldn't be back for a few days, and we went the next day to stay at Grandpa Thomas's, five miles upriver.

The Thomas family had eight generations of family story growing out of one spot between the mountains and the Ohio. A shallow creek — called Stillhouse Run after the moonshining operation that Jed Fankhauser used to run up the holler — ran by the Thomas homeplace. The "Black Irish" — Welsh — Thomases had brown eyes and it was my mother's eyes that showed me the shifting hues of this world. In the sun they gathered off the horizon a topaz glow, and when she was angry they went the orange of the fire in the grate; when she laughed they danced and the irises sparkled with yellow; when she crouched alongside her dogs and gathered them into her embrace her eyes softened to the shade of damp earth. My mother's eyes were just like her father's; they also shared the same olive skin and blue black hair. I believed that those things grew right out of the soil up Stillhouse Run.

When we arrived, Grandpa Thomas was waiting on the porch; without a word he embraced my mother, and her shoulders trembled as she sobbed into his chest. He closed his eyes, then opened them on me. He held my mother for another moment then said, "Jane, go on inside and have some coffee with your mother. I'll walk Jeff down to the river."

Grandpa Thomas stood and watched her go inside and lit a Kool. He blew smoke into the sky, as if in offering, and watched it drift into the breeze. "In ought–two," he told me, "a panther crawled up there" — he crooked a finger at the roof — "all night long, clawin' and tearin' at the roof shakes like it'd drop straight through the roof and come on inside." Finally his father had lit a fire in the chimney and the panther ambled off the roof and back up Sykes Mountain.

The Ohio was only half a mile away. As we walked beneath sycamores and hemlocks, I breathed deep the smell of dampness, and all that rot and blossoming. I wanted to roll up my trousers and work my toes into the mud. But Grandpa wanted to talk. "Your momma, when she was a young'un, would bring in from the Run buckets of crawdads and sell them, a dime a bushel, for fish bait.

"She come by it honest enough," he went on. "My people hadn't been in this country a year" — they migrated to the Ohio Valley in 1811 — "when they lit out for these parts, and this place has been good to us." For generations the Thomas men had piloted riverboats, or built them.

In that holler ringed by mountains the sun went away early even in June. Back on the homeplace, beside the barn, my grandfather gathered his coonhounds about him. With his own voice he could incite those hounds to howl: their treeing voice, he called it. I high-stepped through the rhubarb patch to the brooder house and leaned against the damp stone foundation. My grandfather stood silhouetted in the center of a circle of gleaming beagles, blueticks, and black-and-tans, his profile and theirs pointing to the orange and lavender skies of twilight, as those plaintive harmonies echoed up the holler while fireflies twinkled as if they would foreshadow the stars. We listened to the whippoorwills as the dog star came up right where the sun was.

Before the dark came down I wandered back to Stillhouse Run; already at the age of four a dreaming and distracted child, I laid out on that creek's bank, as I laid there the creek became a river, the river itself became sea, and the boy sprawled face first on the bank became whatever the water wanted: he became whippoorwill, became salamander, became panther.

And always there was the river: the way the creeks swelled as they neared it, the way the river itself moved anew as it gathered them into its body. Whatever imagining a river does must foresee the new shape earth and water will assume with its passage: the shoreline it will remeld, the different earth the water will braid into its body and deliver to some other shore, the soil and sand and deadwood it will drift and hump to shape some new island; and does this river imagine what new life might arise on the turtle shell of that island?

We lived in a battered house trailer that stood precariously perched on cinder blocks; in high winds the roof had a tendency to come loose. In the early '60s things were changing in our remote village: outsiders we called "foreigners" — that is, people who came from beyond the mountains — had started to come in droves along with the aluminum and chemical plants on our stretch of the Ohio. The paternalistic factory chiefs in Pittsburgh and Hartford must have thought hillbillies would be pliant if "slow" laborers who would need "sophisticated" outsiders to oversee their work.

The "foreigners" drove up property values, with their identical split-level Lincoln Houses. My father's parents, who had lived a hundred yards away from our trailer, could no longer afford to live there. The same month that we moved to Schupbach Addition, they moved to Woodsfield, twenty-five miles from the river, where there were no factories and few outsiders.

Grandpap Smith had been raised in a cabin along the river and he'd gone to work in the mine at fifteen. He'd never had time, he'd tell you, for such childish sports as swimming or football; he would count for you the idle days of his life on the coal-stained fingers of one hand. Grandpap wasn't utterly honest — he rarely was — but the point was well-taken: he'd had a rough life, the kind of rough country life that the postwar years wanted to erase from memory.

Early on, my dad started to work himself away from that life. He piloted a ferry boat across the river before he was old enough to drive; he walked the three miles to the ferry after school, and back again at midnight. I was a shotgun baby, born six months after my parents graduated from River High School, my mother the class valedictorian and my father an All-State quarterback. Both were offered college scholarships, but they were married by a justice of the peace and the next day my dad went to work pumping gas and doing mechanic work at Ed's Esso, the only filling station in our town of five hundred.

My dad worked as if possessed. The town knew him as the son of a shiftless miner whose kids spent half-years at a time on relief because the old man couldn't hold a job. My dad could have made more money working in the mines, but he never went back after his first day underground when he felt so claustrophobic that he nearly suffocated. "The Smith men got coal dust in our veins," Grandpap Smith often said — my dad's older brothers were fourth generation miners — "but Bobby's got a yellow streak in his."

But in 1964, the Mobay Chemical Corporation opened a plant five miles from our trailer, and my dad left Ed's to start work with the first batch of laborers Mobay hired. Within two years he was a foreman. In May of 1967, when I was six, we moved into a new suburban-style home in Schupbach Addition, the white-collar neighborhood, half a mile from the trailer where my parents had lived since they were married.

By the time I started school half the kids in my class were "town kids" from outside the region whose fathers were "boss men" at the factories. The natives were the "hill kids" whose families lived up in the mountains away from the river, the way white people there had for generations: mining or working the steep land. Many of their fathers also labored in the factories, swapping the farms and mines for a steady income. The hill kids bore long bus rides to school, wore hand-me-downs, and brought into the classroom the rich scent of the barnyard. They had dirty hands, and the town kids' hands — including my own — were always clean. I doubt that my father went to school with clean hands. But I did. And my clothes were clean and always pressed. But I preferred the company of the hill kids, and went to their farms to spend overnights.

And I was grouped with the hill kids when the Appalachian Regional Commission — a "Great Society" agency whose idea of bettering life in the region was to train us to live somewhere else — sent around buses equipped with language labs and speech therapists to train us to speak standard American English, so that our tongues wouldn't betray our origin when we left for the great American marketplace.

The spring that we moved, the Army Corps of Engineers announced it would commence the following spring to construct a dam on the Ohio, virtually in our front yard. As if in protest a bridge fell into the Ohio some thirty miles downstream, plunging fifteen cars into the water. A great flood came right after construction of the dam started and washed the coffer dams away, delaying completion by three or four years.

The month we moved, I stared at the Ohio out the window of my new bedroom, and I watched it rain, every single day. I was sure all that rain had something to do with our moving. The whole world looked different to me. We had plunked ourselves down a few feet away from absolute strangers who lived in houses identical to ours. The floors were covered with carpet the color of unhealthy moss, and the furniture was protected with plastic slipcovers. We didn't put in a garden. I remember staring out that rain-streaked window, hating my name for its ordinariness, and hoping the river would flood again.

I never thought of my father's miseries, or of his accomplishments. He had come up in the world. His father had never owned a house, and Dad was a "boss man" now, paid a salary and working straight days, off on the weekends. I can only wonder about the guilt and ambivalence he must have felt. Grandpap Smith had been a union agitator in the bitter and bloody "wars" to unionize the mines in the 1930s; he would hear, a few years later, that my father was a company man so despised by the rank and file that they locked him inside Mobay's plant during strikes and phoned our house with threats so specific that we were forced to hide out at a distant cousin's.

And having left the farm and the mine, there was no meaningful work for my dad to teach me. Our world was changing, and it was left to my mother to show me how to fend in it. Before I started school, she taught me to read, and on our walks she helped me catch lizards, turtles, insects, and put them in terrariums when we returned home; I'd watch them for hours. My favorites were the praying mantises: I loved their felid-shaped heads, the way they would gather into their angled and supplicant limbs any cricket or fly I would release into their vicinity, and raise that bounty slowly into their mouths. My first grade teacher called my mother shortly after the start of the school with a worried observation, one that made my mother proud: "Jeff spends all his time at recess staring down into the grass, playing with insects."

This is what I did as a child, while the world outside changed its shape and tenor: I read; I plunged into creeks and overturned rocks on the banks; I walked in the woods and studied on the creatures of the ground.

Eventually this raised suspicions about my paternity. When I was eleven, my dad took up motocross racing, and within a year he was the champion of our district. I was compelled to go to the races and I stuffed cotton batting in my ears against the bikes' din and packed a half-dozen books to take into the woods. After one district championship race, I emerged from the woods with my books soon after silence fell across the race course. My father had won again and gathered with a group of admirers under a tree. I congratulated Dad in some underhearty fashion intended to convey my disgust with the whole enterprise, and sat down on the grass and opened a book. My brother — who as if to disprove Grandpap Smith's genetic theories was born with brown eyes but turned out to be very much my father's son — served on Dad's pit crew even at age nine, and he glared at me. "Who is this," asked one of my dad's comrades, pointing in my direction, "the milkman's son?"

One Sunday when there were no races, we were visiting Stillhouse Run and, coming back down the holler from a long walk, I heard a clanging noise. I neared my grandparents' house and saw my father and brother taking turns dropping one large flat stone onto another. From that distance there was no apparent purpose to this. I came nearer and hid myself behind a sycamore trunk. On the bottom rock lay the carcass of a large blacksnake — a nonpoisonous species welcomed by local farmers because of their appetite for rodents — smashed nearly beyond recognition. From the bottom stone a stream of blood runneled into Stillhouse Run, and still my father and brother went on dropping the stone onto the snake.

My sympathies were — and still are — with the snake. I believed then that this is what became of men who consorted primarily with machines. I know how narrow this view was, and now I attribute my dad's cruelty to his frustration at the way his life had conspired to alienate him from creation.

The distance between us grew broader. In May of 1976, on my weekly visit to the New Martinsville public library, I'd pulled from the shelf a volume of Fitzgerald's short stories. Soon I made my way through all of Fitzgerald's work, and Willa Cather, and Hemingway; then and on through high school I was the only person I knew who read such writers, and this made me arrogant: I must not belong, I thought, in this backwards netherland.

On the Pittsburgh "album rock" station that cable brought into our house, I discovered music. I bought a cheap stereo, and lined up beside it albums I special ordered or shoplifted from McCrory's Five and Dime and Fisher's Big Wheel: Jackson Browne, Neil Young, Bob Dylan. I read *Rolling Stone,* discovered Hunter Thompson, and considered myself tuned into whatever was left, by the mid-70s, of the counterculture.

In short, I copped an attitude. Things were happening "out there," and I set my compass in that direction. I became a "foreigner" in a different way: I determined that my future — what any adolescent calls his or her life — lay outside that valley and those mountains, and I took up residency in those fantasies. I started to plot my escape from that valley's lid of humidity and smog.

I graduated high school in 1980 and became the first person in my family to attend college. I couldn't get out of those hollers fast enough. Right off I became an educated fool, and I didn't see how that place and those people could tell me anything I needed to know. It's taken me years to learn what my father knew the day he threw his father into the river: one must name the shape that betrayal means to create, not just what it will destroy. In the story I clung to, I was the victim. I lacked the courage and the imagination to wedge another story between me and my wound, to create my own life; I lacked the vision to see whatever on heaven and on earth might shape me.

If I can claim any long faithfulness it is to water and to skins, to the rivers I've lived along and the animals I've imagined myself into. We take our fathers where we can find them — we seek them and invent them relentlessly, even into our adulthood.

As a child I sought lessons in rivers, in trees, in animals. As an adult, I sought my lessons in books and in rock and roll; it was a long time before I would listen to anything else. When I was twenty-five, I moved up the "hillbilly highway" — U.S. 23 North — out of Appalachia to the Detroit area. It was the first time I'd been outside the Southern mountains for more than a week. I moved there through a fevered scape of concrete, steel, and glass; I worked nights in an auto parts factory and spent my days working towards a Ph.D. I'm not sure that I wanted to do these things; I did them because they looked like the way out of that holler, away from my father. When I had the time — and increasingly, when I didn't — I was stoned; but that was okay, I rationalized, because my dad didn't smoke pot.

These escapes led nowhere. One sleepless July night I fell onto the banks of the Huron River. It was a landscape like none I had known:

the earth trembled from the airplanes overhead, and there was no birdsong, no fireflies. You may think it was the drugs, or insanity, but I tell you that on that night the Huron River spoke to me. It said: you are not at home here, and will never be. Leave, or die. I listened; I returned to Stillhouse Run.

The month before, Grandpa Thomas had suffered a series of strokes. His left leg had to be amputated, and his general condition was so poor when he left the hospital that his doctors gave him six months to live. A nursing home was out of the question; he wanted to die on his homeplace, so I moved into their house to help my Grandma care for him.

By day, he watched out his window as Stillhouse Run flowed through the homeplace, his brown eyes liquid and expressive as a dog's. He would not sleep; he didn't want to waste his waning light, so he spent the nights telling me stories. Generally by first light he would exhaust himself; his head would drop onto his chest, and I'd lift the cigarette from his fingers and go walking.

The June morning he died, eighteen months later, was cool and sun washed, the sky clear and cirrus-drifted. I set out up the holler on the old dirt two-track, walking past thickets of honeysuckle and chokecherry and sumac.

I crested a rise; bent over a puddle on the trail below was a mother coyote with a pup. I'd never seen a coyote before. Her cinnamon and gray pelage floated with the breeze. She saw me but she didn't move; our gazes fixed each other in place. Her eyes softened to the color of bone. I dropped onto my knees, spread my palms in the mud, and gazed back at her through the Queen Anne's Lace. She offered a quick low bark in my direction and then upended time itself: she held my gaze for an eternity.

She lifted her head then and issued forth a long disconsolate howl that she raised by its coda into an abandoned, rapturous yip that danced in the holler's clear air and echoed down the creek bed all the way to the Ohio. Somehow I knew what it foretold. Directly, I turned back down the holler. I crossed the footbridge over Stillhouse Run and walked through the house straight into Grandpa Thomas's room.

"Set down here," he said to me. He grasped my hand as if he'd mingle our palm prints.

Then his grip slacked. I bent over and put my cheek to his. Against my ear the dry rasping breaths slowed down and grew steady, easy, and full of release. I still believe that coyote's howl was my grandfather's final story to me; I believe that she recognized a kindred soul migrating to the spirit world, and I believe she sang his soul into the afterlife. I pulled away from his cheek, and put my mouth onto his. His last breath landed in my lungs.

On my 29th birthday I drove from Asheville, North Carolina, to West Virginia to have dinner with my father. Before the salad arrived, he told me: "I don't like your hair, I don't like your job, I don't like your clothes, I don't like your life." I tried to lighten the moment by asking if anything about me pleased him; did he like my eyes? I neglected to mention — I'm not sure I was aware of it — that my life was constructed precisely so he wouldn't like it, and so it wouldn't resemble his. I lived in a remote mountain cabin; I managed a homeless shelter; I was an environmental journalist.

But I was involved also with an intelligent and kindred woman and I departed from my dad only by not hitting her: I did everything else I could to control her. As our affair ground on, in the mirror my father's greased, defeated face shone back at me like a talisman, the raging threats fixed in the brow, the lips clasped thin to hold them tight against the teeth. And when I got up close to study these changes, my father's sour, yeasted breath steamed the mirror.

The first panther came soon after, a sepia wash flowing across a swale with its tail snaking behind like wood smoke. Even in the dream, it was utterly silent, utterly self-contained. It came night after night, its eyes clapping themselves to my brow, socketed in their pinioned trackings and flashing through the dark like polestars to navigate by.

I didn't know how to read this dream, so in March I slept beneath a sandstone overhang along the Catawba River and I decided there to let the dream interpret me: I should leave that whole humid quarter, where I hung heavy with self-pity; I should name what I want and hurl myself at it.

I came to Missoula five months later. That Christmas, I left my bike leaning against an outhouse and hiked into the Rattlesnake Wilderness right after dawn. I turned off the ski trail and slogged up a gulch through calf-high snow; up the mountain the trail doglegged away from the creek and started into switchbacks. In the oxbow I saw the ridged taildrags first and followed them to the gaited stalking tracks. The paw prints, long and broad as my palm, gained fast on the unmistakable cloven sign of mule deer. Three long leaps and there was the crimson holograph of battle, the blood weltered and spread like berrystains across the snow.

The deep drag marks went along the creek and north, towards cover or kittens. I didn't follow them. I kneeled there in the stillness. I splayed my arms, scythed them into the snow, and lifted the bloodspoor to my lips. It tasted true. A bell rang beneath my sternum and straightened my limbs, and my shape cast the same shade to earth that the cottonwoods spread into the sky.

I wonder now if out of some urge to forge a link with my dad I've invented this tale about him throwing his dad into the Ohio; the two of them were close, as far as I can tell, before and after that day. In 1975 my dad taught Grandpap Smith to golf, and the two of them traveled each winter to Myrtle Beach for golfing vacations. Grandpap Smith died in 1979 from black lung and cirrhosis, and my dad, alone of all his brothers, wept. Five years later he banished me from his house for some months because I had spoken ill of his father.

These days, Dad and I scarcely speak. There is no animosity; we are mostly tender and friendly with one another, but there is little for us to talk about, no set of shared obsessions or avocations to while away our time together.

My dad has held the same job, and he's lived in that Schupbach Addition house, for thirty years. He's a year past fifty now, survived two heart attacks and continues, as his dad did, to smoke and to drink a 12-pack every day of his life. He's the highest ranking employee at Mobay without a college degree. I called him on his birthday in June and he told me that he plans to retire on his 55th birthday. I was surprised; I wondered how he'd know himself without his work. But I think I understand: Dad's early retirement is his fare-thee-well to the way he has been haunted and driven by his father. He has nothing left to prove. He tells me he's going to become a consultant, and a freelance teacher after he retires; he'll only work when he wants to. Dad knows himself well enough to invent his own life. He's been doing it for years; it started the day he dumped his father into the river. I just haven't noticed.

My neighbors — all those white-collar "foreigners" — and their kids are long gone. The acid rain legislation of the late 1970s closed most of the local mines and gave the area factories that burned the coal an excuse to relocate to right-to-work states. The "hill kids" are mostly still in the valley; they work as bank tellers and barbers, mechanics and stock boys, and none of them farms.

My father can look out his bedroom window and see where that dock once stood. My brother, who works as a diesel mechanic and is my dad's best friend, lives in a trailer park on the other side of the river, and can see that same spot from his back stoop.

My mother, who divorced my dad in 1982, lives on a remote ridge top overlooking the Ohio. My stepfather's family settled that ridge top in the 1830s. Looking west and north she can see my dad's house — our old family home — and my brother's trailer; but for a bend in the Ohio she would see all the way to Stillhouse Run, where my Grandma Thomas still lives.

I think my mother knew all along that the education she gave me would lead me away from that valley: "I wanted to give you roots, and I wanted to give you wings," she has said to me, and I'm struck by her selflessness. She wonders how I can live in a place that virtually lacks mantids and salamanders, and she must wonder how that boy connects with this man.

But she understands about the panthers, and I suspect she knows how the Ohio that she sees every day from her ridge top joins with the Clark Fork that flows beyond my backyard in Missoula: this is the article of faith her father passed to her and she passed to me, in the same blood that braided for some century and a half with the waters that flowed across her old homeplace into the Ohio.

On the Solstice this year, I gather lupine flowers and the buds of wild roses from the banks of the Clark Fork. I bundle them with dried wild azaleas and mountain laurel flowers I'd brought West from the Carolina mountains, and I lay this bouquet into a turtle shell I'd found years before up Stillhouse Run. I kneel there beside the Clark Fork and ask the river to take my offering and braid it into its body.

As the shell drifts down through the rapids to settle on the riverbed, I remember that June afternoon thirty years ago. When we started walking home Grandpap hoisted me onto his shoulders, groped in his tackle box, and handed me a warm Iron City.

My father walked a few feet ahead of us and ignored the cans cracking open. Grandpap cackled as I took my first long draught of beer. "Look at this'un," he said to my dad's back. "Hey Bob. Look at this'un. He is sure as shit one of us. Watch that ole Iron City disappear. Hell, he looks more like me than you do. Look at this'un, Bob. I'll bet he'll never do to his old man what you done to me, Bob. How you've broke my heart."

I turned my head away from my dad and looked back, across the corn growing on the flood plain, towards the Ohio. I looked ahead again, up to the low mountains that ringed the valley. I gazed at those hills shining in the dusk as my dad went on walking, his eyes cast to the ground before his feet. I guzzled the beer down to the dregs and tossed the empty can between cornrows.

Surely I couldn't imagine then that I'd ever want to live out of reach of those hills, in some place where I couldn't hear the Ohio sing down out of the mountains and wash the valleys clean even while we slept. I don't yet feel at home here in the West. So I watch the bouquet drift downriver and ask the Clark Fork to carry to me the blood knowledge that comes from shifting from form to form and from shape to shape, just like any river. I stand on the shore of this river, and I wait for it to show me what shape to take next; I make notes into the palm of my hand, and wait by this river for my next skin; I wait by this west flowing river, to be changed.

Signs of Water

The symbols below, used throughout the book, variously relate to water and its forms. They are only a few of the many, but the themes are fairly standard and repeat across cultures and time.

Based on the signs for water and vessel, this symbol stands for the process of purification, as does the next, more elaborate version.

This means bowl or vessel — a container for water. In this case, we have a lack of water.

Wavy lines signify water in most cultures.

This Late Assyrian (c. 650 BC) representation is water on its way to the abstraction of alphabets and words.

Earlier (c. 2,400 BC), water had this cuneiform symbol.

Those wavy lines again in this pictographic version (c. 3,000 BC).

This pictograph stood for a well.

This is water waving goodbye as it evaporates.

More waves, more water. The triple often means flowing water.

 A minimalist water wave? No, this is a ringer: sand waves.

 Ice, but not necessarily hard water.

 Water in motion: eddies

Water in motion: breakers.

Bios

Marusya Bociurkiw is a feminist/lesbian activist, writer, and film/video maker. Her creative writing has been widely published in journals and anthologies, including *Fireweed*, *Dykewords*, *Queer Looks*, and *The Journey Prize Anthology*. She has produced and directed over a dozen videos and films, among them *Unspoken Territory*, *Night Visions*, and *Bodies in Trouble*, which are screened internationally. Marusya has recently toured a multimedia presentation, "Cross Sexing the Narrative." Born in Alberta of Ukrainian descent, she currently makes Vancouver. B.C., her home.

William deBuys' essay in *Head/Waters* is from his forthcoming book, *Salt Dreams: Reflections from the Downstream West*, a collaboration with photographer Joan Myers, which is under contract to University of New Mexico Press. He is S.W. Representative of The Conservation Fund and edits *Common Ground*, a national newsletter on land and water conservation. Writer of articles, reviews, and stories, his books include *Enchantment and Exploitation: the Life and Hard Times of a New Mexico Mountain Range* and *River of Traps: a Village Life*, both published by University of New Mexico Press. The latter was the 1991 finalist for the Pulitzer Prize for General Non-Fiction.

David James Duncan is the author of two novels, *The River Y* and *The Brothers K*. His collection of stories will be published by Doubleday in 1995. He contributed work to *Gotta Earn A Living*, the third title released by Left Bank Books. He lives on a fine stretch of water near Lolo Pass, Montana.

Ed Edmo was raised at Celilo Falls, Oregon, a traditional Indian fishing site on the Columbia River. He feels that watching the river's flow helped give him the cadence of his poetry. "The river was a welcome playmate that never got called in for supper," he says. Ed is a poet, playwright, short story writer, and traditional storyteller as well as an actor. His award-winning one-man show, "Through Coyote's Eyes: A Visit With Ed Edmo" deals with racism, alcoholism, and child abuse in a quiet, situational way. His poetry has been published internationally, including *These Few Words of Mine* (Blue Cloud Press) and his short story "After Celilo," which appears in *Talking Leaves* (Dell).

Lorian Hemingway, half-Cherokee, was raised in the South and worked as a freelance journalist for twenty years. Publications include feature pieces in *Rolling Stone*, *New York Times Sunday Magazine*, *Sports Afield*, *Chicago Tribune*, *Washington Post*, and *Miami Herald*. Her first novel, *Walking Into the River*, published by Simon & Schuster, 1992, was subsequently published in nine foreign countries and nominated for the Mississippi Arts and Letters Award for Fiction, 1993. Lorian was Director of the Hemingway Short Story Competition for fifteen years. "I was once a swimming pool cleaner so I could be near water."

Pam Houston's story "Selway" is excerpted from her book *Cowboys Are My Weakness*. She is a part-time river guide and hunting guide, and is finishing her Ph.D. at the University of Utah. Pam has published in *Mirabella, Mademoiselle, Cimarron Review,* and *Gettysburg Review.*

Aaron Johanson: "I appeared in Portland in 1958. I grew up and received the majority of my education in Oregon but spent the last third of my life living, working, and photographing abroad. My prolonged stay abroad has expanded my horizons, while not at all diminishing my attachment to Oregon. From 1995 on, I plan to reverse the ratio of my published work: six-sevenths from Oregon, one-seventh from Japan."

George Johanson lives in Portland, Oregon. He taught painting and printmaking at the Pacific Northwest College of Art for 25 years, and was a founding member of the Northwest Print Council and its first president 1981–83. George is represented in Portland by the Elizabeth Leach Gallery.

The author of two short story collections, including *Survival,* **Nancy Lord** is currently working on a book about the human and natural history surrounding her fish camp in Alaska. Her essays have appeared in *Sierra, Manoa, Alaska Quarterly Review,* and in the first two Left Bank Books collections. "I value the wild salmon and the clean, unobstructed, teeming-with-life habitat on which they depend, and I'm active in marine conservation work. My hero is Rachel Carson."

Jessica Maxwell is a columnist based on an island in Puget Sound, Washington. She is currently working on a Northwest fishing book and a documentary film about salmon.

Ellen Meloy is an artist, writer, and native of the West. Her essays have appeared in the anthology, *Montana Spaces,* published by Lyons in 1989, and a variety of periodicals, including *Northern Lights, Utne Reader,* and *Harper's.* For most of the year she works with her husband as a river ranger in a remote redrock canyon in southern Utah. That canyon is the subject of her first book, *Raven's Exile: a Season on the Green River* published by Holt in 1994. Her essay in *Head/Waters* is from that book. She winters in Montana.

Ken Olsen is not lobbying for a Surgeon General's warning on drinking water though he is frequently accused of packing a water-filter pump into restaurants. Otherwise, he wets his whistle with purified ale, writes for newspapers, and freelances as often as possible.

Brenda Peterson, born in 1950, spent much of her childhood moving around the country following her father's U.S. Forest Service work. She is the author of three novels: *River of Light,* Knopf, 1978; *Becoming the Enemy,* Graywolf Press, 1988; and *Duck and Cover,* HarperCollins, 1991, which was selected as *New York Times* "Best Book of 1992." Brenda has two collection of essays: *Living by Water,* Alaska Northwest Books, 1990, just out in paperback from Fawcett, and *Nature and Other Mothers,* Harper Collins, 1992. She has spent the last twelve years on the shores of Puget Sound, and has just finished her sixth book, *Sister Stories,* to be published by Viking/Penguin, 1995.

Marc Reisner enjoys white water boating, stream and ocean fishing, mountaineering, piano, jazz, and billiards. A native of Minnesota, he graduated from Richmond, Indiana's Earlham College with degrees in history and politics, disciplines put to good use in researching and writing his three books, *Cadillac Desert, Game Wars,* and *Overtapped Oasis.* In addition to his work as a lecturer and environmental consultant, he is working on his fourth book, a contemporary history of California, which, with tongue in cheek, he says ought to be entitled *The Bonfire of the Vanity Plates.*

Rick Rubin grew up in a gray stucco house 180 feet above sea level, and lives now in a blue house 110 feet above sea level. The houses are only about a kilometer apart, but it was the 36 years of freelance writing that depressed him those 70 feet. He has written every kind of stuff: Sunday magazine features, essays both personal and impersonal, ad copy, fiction and nonfiction books, industrial journalism, short stories, columns, disaster scenarios, and impassioned letters. He always keeps his life preserver close at hand, and urges all who will listen, "Mothers, don't raise your child to be a freelance writer."

Joan Skogan has worked as an observer for the Canadian Fisheries Department since 1987. Her short fiction and memoirs have appeared in publications such as *Grain*, *West Coast Review*, and *Saturday Night*. Her books include: most recently *Voyage At Sea With Strangers*, Harper & Collins International, 1994; and from Polestar Press: *Skeena A River Remembered; The Princess and the SeaBear and other Trimshian Stories*; and *Grey Cat at Sea*.

Jeffery Smith lives in Missoula, Montana. "Shapeshifting" is his first published essay.

Gary Snyder grew up in rural Washington, attending high school in Seattle and Portland. He did graduate study in Oriental Languages, became a researcher and translator of Zen Buddhist texts, and lived in Japan for twelve years. Gary is identified with the Beat Generation and associated with Allen Ginsberg, Kenneth Rexroth, and Jack Kerouac. He has published fifteen books of poetry and prose; *Turtle Island* won the Pulitzer prize for poetry in 1975. [I am] "working with my local watershed group, the Yuba Watershed Council, on a joint-management agreement for a sizable parcel of BLM land in our area that we call the Inimim forest. It is an instructive hands-on exercise in fledgling ecosystem management."

After years of being landlocked in the desert southwest as an artist and curator at the Museum of Fine Arts in Santa Fe, **Susan Zwinger** lives and floats about Whidbey Island, Washington. She is a full-time natural history writer. "Becoming Water" originally appeared in the *Island Independent*, a journal of the rain shadow in Washington State and British Columbia.

LEFT BANK BOOKS
A NEW WAY TO READ BETWEEN THE LINES

WRITING & FISHING THE NORTHWEST — Consider the cast. Wallace Stegner, Greg Bear, Craig Lesley, Sharon Doubiago, Nancy Lord, John Keeble. #1. ISBN 0-936085-19-3; $7.95.

EXTINCTION — Get it before it's gone. David Suzuki introduces Tess Gallagher, Barry Lopez, David Quammen, Sallie Tisdale, Robert Michael Pyle, John Callahan, Nancy Lord, and others. #2. ISBN 0-936085-50-9; $7.95.

SEX, FAMILY, TRIBE — Get intimate with Ursula Le Guin, Ken Kesey, William Stafford, Colleen McElroy, Matt Groening, William Kittredge, Charles Johnson, and many more. #3. ISBN 0-936085-53-5; $7.95.

GOTTA EARN A LIVING — Know the work of two baker's dozen, including Norman Maclean, Kate Braid, Gary Snyder, David James Duncan, Teri Zipf, Sherman Alexie, Sibyl James, and Robin Cody. #4. ISBN 0-936085-54-1; $7.95.

BORDER & BOUNDARIES — Flee with the Bedouins, secede from the Union, travel with Michael Dorris, Diana Abu-Jaber, William Stafford, Sandra Scofield, Larry Colton. #5. ISBN 0-936085-58-4; $9.95.

KIDS' STUFF — Definitely not for kids. Enjoy Mikal Gilmore, Sallie Tisdale, Sherman Alexie, Ann Rule, Virginia Euwer Wolff, Shani Mootoo, and others. #6. ISBN 0-936085-26-6; $9.95.

BOOKSTORES, SEE COPYRIGHT PAGE FOR ORDERING INFORMATION. INDIVIDUALS, PHOTOCOPY THE ORDER FORM ON THE LAST PAGE, OR ASK FOR LEFT BANK BOOKS AT YOUR FAVORITE BOOKSTORE.

LEFT BANK BOOKS
GREAT WRITING
GREAT READING
GREAT GIFTS
ORDER HERE

For yourself or any thoughtful friend.

Just photocopy this page, fill in the form below, and send it today. Subs are $16, postage paid, and begin with the next book to be published. Other titles are available; add $2.50 shipping for the first book and 75¢ for each additional book.

Send Left Bank to me at:

Send a gift subscription to:

I'd like the following editions (see previous page):

My order total is:

I've enclosed a check ☐ or Money Order ☐ — or charge my VISA ☐ or MC ☐; its number and expiration are:

VISA/MC orders may be placed at 503.621.3911 or mailed to Blue Heron Publishing, 24450 NW Hansen Road, Hillsboro, OR 97124.